D<small>IN</small>EFENSE <small>OF</small> ISRAEL

JOHN HAGEE

FRONT LINE

A STRANG COMPANY

Most Strang Communications/Charisma House/Siloam/FrontLine/ Realms products are available at special quantity discounts for bulk purchase for sales promotions, premiums, fund-raising, and educational needs. For details, write Strang Communications/Charisma House/Siloam/FrontLine/Realms, 600 Rinehart Road, Lake Mary, Florida 32746, or telephone (407) 333-0600.

In Defense of Israel by John Hagee
Published by FrontLine
A Strang Company
600 Rinehart Road
Lake Mary, Florida 32746
www.frontlineissues.com

Unless otherwise noted, all Scripture quotations are from the New King James Version of the Bible. Copyright © 1979, 1980, 1982 by Thomas Nelson, Inc., publishers. Used by permission.

Scripture quotations marked kjv are from the King James Version of the Bible.

Scripture quotations marked nas are from the New American Standard Bible. Copyright © 1960, 1962, 1963, 1968, 1971, 1972, 1973, 1975, 1977 by the Lockman Foundation. Used by permission. (www.Lockman.org)

Scripture quotations marked niv are from the Holy Bible, New International Version. Copyright © 1973, 1978, 1984, International Bible Society. Used by permission.

Quotations from the Quran are from The Quran Translation, seventh edition, by Abdullah Yusef Ali (Elmhurst, NY: Tahrike Tarsile Quran, Inc., 2001).

Cover design by Marvin Eans
Executive Design Director: Bill Johnson

Library of Congress Cataloging-in-Publication Data
Hagee, John.
  In defense of Israel / John Hagee. -- 1st ed.
      p. cm.
  Includes bibliographical references and index.
  ISBN 978-1-59979-210-1
  1. Israel (Christian theology) 2. Christianity and other
religions--Judaism. 3. Judaism--Relations--Christianity. I. Title.
  BT590.J8H34 2007
  231.7'6--dc22

                              2007028267

First Edition
07 08 09 10 11 — 9 8 7 6 5 4 3 2
Printed in the United States of America

To the regional, state, and local directors of

Christians United for Israel—

dedicated leaders who have taken a bold stand

In Defense of Israel

CONTENTS

FOREWORD

MARCH 12, 2007, WAS A DAY IN TIME AND A MOMENT IN history. Televangelist preacher John Hagee spoke to six thousand of the most prominent, sophisticated Jewish leaders of the United States, and perhaps the world, at the American Israel Public Affairs Committee (AIPAC) Convention. His passionate words and his grasp of world affairs electrified the audience and transformed them into friends and, above all, believers in the cause of Christian support for Israel and Jewish people.

The Jewish audience saw in the person of Pastor John Hagee Christian friendship, Christian sacrifice, and unwavering Christian support in the defense of Israel and the Jewish people.

It was a moment in history because his embrace of love redeemed millennia of Jewish martyrdom.

For many years, Pastor Hagee has lived and labored selflessly for the people of Israel. In 1981, when the world condemned Israel for bombing a nuclear reactor in Iraq, Pastor Hagee's response to world critics for Israel was to start "A Night to Honor Israel." That night Pastor Hagee proclaimed, "Israel, you are not alone; Christians support you, and America supports you. We love you, and we shall stand by you." For the last twenty-five years, A Night to Honor Israel has given encouragement, inspiration, and comfort to people who often felt alone. A Night to Honor Israel has also raised millions of dollars to support charities and resettlement of world Jewry in Israel.

In February of 2006, Pastor Hagee started a most ambitious and daring venture to strengthen and support Israel and the Jewish people: Christians United for Israel (CUFI). CUFI has assembled leaders of evangelical Christendom for one purpose alone, to defend and support Israel.

Pastor Hagee's books have sold millions of copies, and his teachings have reached scores of millions of people throughout the world. Pastor Hagee, during this very turbulent time in the world both for Israel and America, has been a clear and wise voice that has alerted the world to the duplicity and hypocrisy of Europe, the United Nations, and the Arab and Muslim countries of the world.

The prophet Isaiah, in chapter 49, verse 22, says, "For thus saith my Lord, behold I will raise my hand toward the nations, and to the peoples will I hoist my banner, and they shall bring your sons in their arms, and your daughters shall be carried on their shoulders. Kings will be your nurturers and their princesses your wet-nurses....For the Lord shall comfort Zion, He shall comfort all of her rooms; He shall make her wilderness like Eden and her wastelands like a garden of the Lord, joy and gladness shall be found there."

The Lord has hoisted his banner to rally his troops. The evangelical Christians under the leadership of Pastor John Hagee have come to the forefront in support and defense of Israel. He has led the cavalry charge to Christendom.

In his new book, *In Defense of Israel,* Pastor Hagee makes a profound and compelling case for defending Israel. I believe it is a must-read and will strengthen and inspire Christians and all lovers of Zion in these defining years of destiny.

—RABBI ARYEH SCHEINBERG

SAN ANTONIO, TEXAS

CHAPTER 1

IT'S 1938...AGAIN

URING DIFFICULT DAYS SUCH AS THIS, WHEN IT SEEMS that the whole world is against Israel, many in the Jewish community nervously scan the globe, searching for friends."

Standing behind the massive gray podium with the blue AIPAC logo, I looked out across the darkened banquet hall. Candlelight flickered from glass containers on the tabletops. Faces were indistinguishable, but I sensed six thousand pairs of eyes scanning the stage. I was well aware that most of the largely Jewish audience disagreed with me on many political issues. But on the issues of the need to support Israel and recognition of the dangerous situation in the Middle East today, we were in total agreement.

"You look toward the United Nations," I continued, "which Ambassador Dore Gold calls 'the Tower of Babble.' You look at Europe, where the ghost of Hitler is again walking across the stage of history. You open your newspapers and read about American universities, where Israel is being vilified by students taught by professors whose Middle Eastern chairs are sponsored by Saudi Arabia. You look to America's mainline churches and see their initiatives to divest from Israel. You go to the bookstore and see slanderous titles by the former president of the United States—and you feel very much alone."

I leaned into the podium, feeling as confident—and as earnest—as if I were addressing my Cornerstone congregation. "I want to say this as clearly and plainly as I possibly can: Israel, you are not alone. Ladies and gentlemen, it's a new day in America. The sleeping giant of Christian Zionism has awakened. Fifty million Christians are standing up and applauding the State of Israel."

Suddenly six thousand people were standing to their feet and applauding the support I offered on behalf of evangelical Christians, whom I was honored to represent as the first pastor ever invited to address the American Israel Public Affairs Committee (AIPAC), the largest and most influential advocacy group for Israel and the Jewish people in the United States.

How I came to be a keynote speaker during the AIPAC 2007 Policy Conference is part of the story of this book. In these pages I want to convey the same message to you that I presented to that audience. It's the message I have been preaching on television and in churches and auditoriums across America for twenty-six years.

As an avid student of history, I am convinced that we are facing the same situation the world faced in 1938.

Iran is the new Germany, and its president, Mahmoud Ahmadinejad, is the new Hitler. Iran poses a threat to the State of Israel that promises nothing less than a nuclear holocaust. The only way to win a nuclear war is to make certain it never starts. We must stop Iran's nuclear threat and stand boldly with Israel, the only democracy in the Middle East.

Millions of evangelicals in America have joined me in Christians United for Israel. We have agreed to set aside our theological and political differences in order to focus on one issue: support for and defense of the nation of Israel and the Jewish people. I can assure you that we will not sit by in silence this time while another maniacal leader plots and plans the destruction of the Jewish people. There will never be another Holocaust—not on our watch. *Never again.*

Just prior to World War II there were obvious and clear warnings that Hitler was moving forward to implement his Final Solution. Winston Churchill tried to warn the forces of appeasement. He said that an appeaser is someone who feeds a crocodile in the futile hope it will eat him last.[1] In 1938 Czechoslovakia's Sudetenland was turned into crocodile food for Germany. The Nazi beast smelled the weakness in the international appeasers and devoured most of Europe, systematically slaughtering six million Jewish people.

What did America do? We debated the situation in Congress, and we let isolationist sentiments keep us from getting involved while millions of innocent people died.

Today, the same warning signs are present and, in the age of mass media, more obvious than ever. Numerous groups calling themselves religions are spouting hateful, racist vitriol, and many observers who should know better are trying to wish the situation away. Every time Israel defends itself, critics cry foul and try to accuse Israel and the United States of wrongdoing. This is history repeating itself.

We are constantly hearing calls to appease the enemies of Israel and the Jewish people. Once again those who would appease seek to do so at the expense of Israel. They tell us that if we want the Sunnis and the Shiites to stop massacring each other in Iraq, then Israel must give up land. They tell us that if we want the Syrians to stop murdering the leaders in Lebanon, then Israel must give up land. They tell us that if we want the Saudis to permit women to drive and to vote, Israel must give up land. If we want the sun to rise in the east and set in the west, Israel must give up land.

Let me be clear: Israel is not the problem, and making Israel the scapegoat will not solve anything. The problem is the rejection of Israel's right to exist. The problem is radical Islam's bloodthirsty embrace of a theocratic dictatorship that believes they have a mandate from God to kill. The problem is the failure of the moderates in the Arab and Muslim world to stand up and rein in these Islamic extremists.

Appeasement is not the answer. Appeasement, as President Eisenhower once said, is nothing more than surrender on the installment plan.[2] The U.S. State Department should not pressure Israel to give up land. America must never pressure Israel to divide the city of Jerusalem, the eternal capital of the Jewish people now and forever.

Speaking of the Jewish people, the Word of God says, "I will bless those who bless you, and I will curse those who curse you" (Genesis 12:3). I believe those blessings—and those judgments—are very real.

But across the world we are hearing voices raised in curses against Israel. Even supposedly devout Christians praise the patriarchs of the past—Abraham, Isaac, and Jacob—while avoiding their Jewish neighbors across the street.

That's anti-Semitism, and anti-Semitism is sin. And as sin, it damns the soul.

As Christians we should ask God's forgiveness and ask the Jewish people for forgiveness of every act of anti-Semitism in our past. The Crusades. The Spanish Inquisition. Martin Luther's "Concerning the Jews and Their Lies." The Final Solution of Adolf Hitler, which was carried out by baptized Christians in good standing with their church.[3]

In 1938 far too many world leaders, including those in the United States, did not take seriously the threat Nazi Germany represented to the Jewish citizens of Europe until millions of innocent lives were lost. There is a pattern throughout history of persecution of the Jewish people around the world, often at the hands of brutal thugs presenting themselves as religious leaders, while the rest of the world feigns ignorance.

The sin of *omission*, the sin of remaining silent bystanders, is just as serious as the sin of *commission*, of actually committing the crime. When we turn a blind eye to an impending atrocity, we are as guilty as the perpetrator of the crime. If we ignore the events in our world today, much as our ancestors ignored them during the reign of the Nazis, we are repeating history in a way that can only be seen as sinful.

Let me point you to the story of Esther to underscore why it is absolutely crucial that Christians defend Israel.

Esther, whose real name was Hadassah, was a young Jewish girl who became the queen of Persia. She had kept her identity secret, but when she learned of an evil plot by a wicked government official to destroy all the Jews living in Persia, Mordecai, the cousin who had raised her, instructed Esther to intercede with the king—knowing it would put her life in danger.

"Do not think," Mordecai said, "that because you are in the king's house you alone of all the Jews will escape. For if you remain silent at this time, relief and deliverance for the Jews will arise from another place, but you and your father's family will perish. And who knows but that you have come to royal position for such a time as this?" (Esther 4:13–14, NIV).

The important message is this: God placed this woman in a critical position to help the Jewish people when an evil man, in this case Haman, was plotting to have the Jews exterminated. This took place in Persia, which is modern Iran.

Today another Persian—Ahmadinejad, the president of Iran—is plotting to exterminate the Jewish people. His goal is to put together the capability for a nuclear holocaust. And God is saying to Christians, just as Mordecai said to Esther, "If you remain silent at this time, I will see to it that deliverance comes to the Jews from another place. But you and your house will perish."

Mark my words: *deliverance will come.*

Deliverance will come to the Jewish people again, even if God himself has to come and save them. But I believe America's evangelicals have been elevated to a position of influence "for such a time as this." If we will defend Israel, God will defend America. But if we remain silent at this very critical time, when the survival of Israel is at stake, I believe the judgment of God will fall on America. The terrorists who live among us can only be prevented by the hand of God.

There is a verse in Matthew 25 that few Christians understand in context. Jesus said to his disciples, "I tell you the truth, whatever you did for one of the least of these brothers of mine, you did for me" (verse 40, NIV).

The expression "these brothers of mine" in this verse is a Greek term that refers to "relatives according to the flesh."

Jesus was speaking about the Jewish people when he said, "I was hungry and you didn't give me food. I was thirsty and you didn't give me water. I was naked and you didn't clothe me."

"When did we see you in that condition?" the disciples asked him.

Jesus replied that it was whenever they saw one of his "relatives" in that condition.

Whenever Christians have seen the relatives of Jesus suffering—for instance, in the Holocaust—and done nothing, it was as if they had ignored the suffering of Christ himself.

Jesus was not asking for emotion from his disciples; he wanted action. He did not tell them, "You didn't feel sorry for me; you didn't weep for me." No, he said, "You didn't *do* anything for me. You did not take action to solve the problem."

This is the only time in Scripture that Jesus asked those who followed him to do something specific for him.

This is the gift that Christ is asking Christians to give to him today: "Do something for my relatives." The Jewish people are still his family. They are still the apple of God's eye. No, they don't see Jesus for who Christians believe he is, but they will in the future. And until then, help them. Have compassion on them. Feed them, clothe them, and protect them. Speak out and *defend them*.

While we look on all of the people in the Middle East with

love and compassion, we cannot ignore the leaders of the radical factions and their lust for the death and destruction of the Jewish people and the nation of Israel. That was my pledge to the Jewish leaders in America at the AIPAC Policy Conference—to pay attention to the threat and to do something about it on behalf of the "relatives" of Jesus.

"Tonight, on this historic occasion," I told the thousands of attendees, "we ask God's forgiveness and yours for every act of anti-Semitism in our past, and for the deafening silence of Christianity in your greatest hour of need during the Holocaust. We were not there; we cannot change the past...

"But together we can shape the future."

In the following pages I will explore the past and look into the future as I lay out the case for the defense of Israel. But first, I want to tell you how I arrived at this position.

And it all started, I suppose, when I was eight years old.

CHAPTER 2

MY LIFELONG LOVE
FOR ISRAEL

BELIEVE IT OR NOT, I WAS A SCRAWNY KID. In fact, when I started elementary school, my mother took me to the doctor to see why I couldn't gain weight. He prescribed a time-honored country remedy: cod liver oil. So every day—for two long years—I had a dose of cod liver oil. It was the vilest stuff I have ever put in my mouth.

My dad had built our home in tiny Channelview, Texas, during the Depression. The kitchen was cramped, with barely enough room for a stove, refrigerator, and sink. When all four of us—my mom, my dad, my brother, Bill, and I—gathered around the dinner table, that kitchen was standing room only.

One almost-summer evening at that square white wooden table stands out in my mind. My skinny legs dangled off the chair, a loose lace on my Buster Brown shoes flapping. While my mother cleaned the kitchen, my father, a quiet, studious man, was reading a book and listening to the evening news. An announcer's voice crackled through the plastic case of the old RCA radio.

Although I loved the Saturday night dramas and comedies, I usually paid scant attention to the news. But the report that Friday night in May 1948 was something I would never forget.

It was the first time I ever saw tears in my father's eyes.

Of course, I don't remember the exact words spoken by the announcer, but the news report would have been taken from this telegram, a copy of which is in the presidential library of Harry Truman:

> A FEW MINUTES AFTER THE PROCLAMATION OF A JEWISH STATE IN PALESTINE BECAME EFFECTIVE AT 6:01 P.M. EDT, MR. TRUMAN ISSUED THIS STATEMENT:
>
> "THIS GOVERNMENT HAS BEEN INFORMED THAT A JEWISH STATE HAS BEEN PROCLAIMED IN PALESTINE, AND RECOGNITION HAS BEEN REQUESTED BY THE PROVISIONAL GOVERNMENT THEREOF.
>
> "THE UNITED STATES RECOGNIZES THE PROVISIONAL GOVERNMENT AS THE DEFACTO AUTHORITY OF THE NEW STATE OF ISRAEL."
>
> 5/14—JM625P[1]

When the announcer said, "the new state of Israel," my father's eyes filled with tears. I knew something momentous had just happened.

Both my parents were Bible scholars, and for all of my eight years I had been in church every time the doors opened. I had heard about Israel over and over—in Bible stories and sermons. Finally, for the first time, it connected with me that there was an actual Israel on this earth. The place my father had so often preached about was real.

I felt the emotion that washed over him. After a moment Dad looked at me and said, "Son, today is the most important day of the twentieth century. God's promise to bring the Jewish people back to Israel is being fulfilled before our eyes."

Dispensational theology was drilled into me from an early age, but it would be many years later—long after I had given up my rebellion against the legalistic religion of my childhood and surrendered to God's calling to enter the ministry—that the real impact of my father's words would become clear to me.

There is a prophecy in Scripture foretelling that a nation will be born in a day. It comes from the Book of Isaiah.

> Who has ever heard of such a thing?
>> Who has ever seen such things?
> Can a country be born in a day
>> or a nation be brought forth in a moment?
>
> —Isaiah 66:8, NIV

The rebirth of Israel as a nation was an unmistakable milestone on the prophetic timetable leading to the return of Christ. Over the years, as I devoted myself to the study of biblical prophecy, the memory of that childhood day in May 1948 grew in significance.

But it was not until I took my first trip to Israel some thirty years later that my interest in Israel blossomed into an abiding love of the nation and its people. In 1978 Diana and I went on a ten-day trip to Israel with our first tour group. We went as tourists and came home as Zionists.[2]

How thrilling it was to walk where Jesus had walked. We visited Tiberias and the Sea of Galilee. We saw Hebron and the Cave of the Patriarchs. We visited Bethlehem, the birthplace of Jesus. We stood on the Mount of Olives and looked over the ancient City of David. But without a doubt, Jerusalem itself was the highlight of our trip.

As I walked the narrow cobblestone streets of the four quarters of the Old City, I felt I had come home. In a way I could never have imagined, I experienced Jerusalem as my spiritual home. For the first time, I fully understood that my spiritual roots were in this place. I have never felt about any other place on the earth as I felt about the city of Jerusalem.

Nor have I had an experience quite like I had at the Kotel, or Western Wall, the ancient retaining wall that dates from 516 B.C., on the Temple Mount. This towering stone wall is the only remnant of the second temple, which was destroyed by Titus and his Roman legions when they sacked the city of Jerusalem in A.D. 70.

The Kotel is the holiest place in Judaism that is accessible to Jewish worshipers. Here tourists mingle with the devout, who come to pray and recite the Torah or to hold their bar mitzvah celebrations, the occasion when Jewish boys turn thirteen, the traditional age of responsibility. Jews believe that the *Shekinah*, the divine presence of God, rests on the Wall.

Men and women cannot pray together at the Kotel, so Diana and I parted ways at the portable divider. At first I stood at a distance from the Wall, amazed at its height and the size of the massive stones. The largest of them, I learned later, weighs 570 tons and is the heaviest object ever to have been lifted by men without the aid of machinery.[3]

As I walked closer, I noticed curling bits of paper wedged in the nooks and crannies between the stones; the tour guide had said these were prayer requests. I opened my Bible and read for a few minutes, and then I leaned against the Wall and began to pray silently. Voices were raised around me, speaking in Hebrew. I recognized only a few words, but the fervor of the prayers was unmistakable.

An elderly man sat nearby in one of the blue plastic chairs available for worshipers. He was reading aloud from the Torah. Dressed in the distinctive garb of the Orthodox Jew—a white shirt and long black coat over black trousers—he had a full beard, and a bead-trimmed yarmulke, or skullcap, was pinned to the top of his head. A white-and-blue shawl lay across his shoulders, and he rocked back and forth as he addressed almighty God.

I was captivated by the sight and sound of this man. "Here we are at the same holy place," I thought, "praying to the same God, believing the same Scriptures. And yet I know nothing about this man or his faith."

For reasons I could not explain, that thought profoundly disturbed me. How could I *not* know what was in his heart or mind? Why did I know so little about the Jewish faith when I could recite long passages of Scripture and engage in theological debates about the meaning of verses penned so many centuries ago—by *Jewish* writers? My faith was connected to this man's. We had shared beliefs and history, yet I was ignorant of the connections of Christianity with Judaism.

Reluctantly, I left the Western Wall and rejoined Diana, who had already finished praying. But I could not get the elderly Jewish man out of my mind. My wife slipped her hand in mine, and we started walking back to the tour bus, which was parked quite a distance from the Kotel. I broke the silence by blurting out, "I believe the Lord wants me to do everything in my power to bring Christians and Jews together."

"What makes you think that?" she asked.

I told her about the man I'd seen praying at the Wall and how it disturbed me that I knew so little about him or his faith. "I want to buy one of those shawls," I said. "I'm not sure why, but it's important."

Diana let me go on for a moment. When I paused, she said, "How would you go about bringing Jews and Christians together? Both are extremely suspicious of the other."

"I don't have the slightest idea," I replied. "I just know I'm supposed to."

The very next stop on our tour happened to be a Jewish store named Harp of David. Inside I found one of the white-and-blue shawls and learned it was called a *tallit,* or prayer shawl. I eagerly bought it, along with $150 worth of books. I had inherited my father's passion for reading and learning, and that day I chose books on the history of Israel and the Jewish people: *The Anguish of the Jews* by Father Flannery; *The War Against the Jew* by Dagobert Runes; and John Toland's two-volume history of Adolf Hitler.

I began reading as soon as we got back on the tour bus, and I continued reading on the flight home. I was a graduate of two secular universities and a Bible college and had been raised in a Christian home all my life, but I had never learned anything close to the truth about what the Jewish people had gone through historically. I read about the Crusades, the Spanish Inquisition, and the Holocaust, probing into the dark abyss of a history I had never been taught.

Somewhere over the Atlantic I began jotting down notes on what I could do to bring Christians and Jews together—without starting a riot. We have not exactly had a cordial relationship over the centuries. What made me think I could possibly change something that had been ingrained in the hearts and minds of these two vastly different groups for two thousand years?

I couldn't, of course. At least not on my own. The important thing was that I recognized it was God who had placed that desire in my heart on the day I had prayed at the Western Wall. The books I had purchased in Jerusalem became the intellectual foundation of my life's work. It would be another three years before I took any specific action toward fulfilling the mission God had given me that day, but the one step I did take was to confront the truth that the fathers of the Christian church had been chief among the persecutors of the Jewish people throughout history.

CHAPTER 3

SINS OF THE FATHERS

THE HISTORY I DISCOVERED IN THE BOOKS I BROUGHT HOME from Israel was unlike anything I had ever learned in my university education. When average Americans hear the term *anti-Semitism*, they probably think of Hitler and the Nazis, or al Qaeda and the militant jihadist terrorist organizations. They might even think about the Ku Klux Klan or "skinheads" right here in the United States. In actuality, anti-Semitism has its origin and its complete root structure in Christianity, dating from the early days of the Christian church. Until we come to terms with the true origins of anti-Semitism, we will not be able to correctly address this most egregious of sins.

The very idea of a Christian anti-Semite is an oxymoron, an absolute contradiction in terms. Anti-Semitism is a synonym for hatred. Christianity is a synonym for love. Show me an anti-Semitic Christian, and I'll show you a spiritually dead Christian whose hatred for other human beings has strangled his faith.

The Christian doctrine of love was first taught by a Jewish rabbi from Nazareth, who said: "Love your neighbor as yourself" (Matthew

19:19, NIV). "Love one another as I have loved you" (John 15:12). "By this all will know that you are My disciples, if you have love for one another" (John 13:35). "Love your enemies" (Matthew 5:44).

Since we know that Jesus taught a doctrine of love, when did the doctrine of hatred toward the Jewish people begin? How did Gentiles and Jews who followed the teachings of Christ in the early church become separated? How did it happen that within three hundred years the church inspired by a Jewish rabbi and his twelve Jewish disciples began to kill Jews as a matter of church policy? Allow me to offer a brief explanation.

Following the crucifixion of Jesus and his resurrection and ascension to heaven, Jewish and Gentile believers continued to worship together in harmony for decades. When Titus marched from Rome in A.D. 70, he laid siege to the city of Jerusalem for months, crippling and eventually destroying the Holy City. Jerusalem was left in ruins, including the center of its faith, the great temple. The massive stones were crushed into rubble, leaving only a portion of the Western Wall, which became known by Gentiles as the Wailing Wall because of the deep mourning of the Jewish people at the loss of their temple. More than one million Jews died during the Roman siege of Jerusalem; most of them starved to death.

The majority of the remaining 97,000 Jews were taken back to Rome, where many were crucified on Roman crosses while their wives and children were forced to watch. Some were martyred in one of the many stadiums in Rome. Seventy thousand were enslaved and forced to build the Roman Colosseum.

Many Gentile believers fled Jerusalem for the nearby city of Pella to escape the attack, while the Jews remained behind. Why did the Gentiles leave? They had heard Jesus say that Jerusalem would be attacked, that there would be "wars and rumors of war," and he advised them to flee to the mountains (Matthew 24). When the Romans gave the Gentiles the option of leaving Jerusalem, they did exactly that. This physical separation of the two groups would prove to be permanent and would form the basis of the strained relationship between them.

The Jews saw the Gentile exodus as a betrayal, and the breach between the two groups was never repaired. This separation of Jews and Gentiles became official early in the fourth century, when the emperor Constantine "Christianized" the Roman Empire. In one day, with one swing of his pen, he made Rome's version of Christianity the official state religion, a religion full of idolatry because of pagan influence. It was known in history as the mother-child cult and in ancient Israel as Baal worship, which was introduced by Jezebel.

The monotheistic theology of the devout Jews was more than Rome could understand and certainly more than it would tolerate. Rome had a pantheon of gods and disdained the Jews' loyalty to only one deity. The Roman consensus was that the Jews were simply stubborn, rebellious people, when in fact the Jewish people were keeping the first commandment.

> Constantine and his clergymen at the Council of Nicea quickly began enacting a series of restrictive edicts against the Jewish people. His purpose was to separate the Gentiles and Jews from worshipping together. In his words, he considered the Jews an "evil and perverse sect...let us have nothing to do with the Jews who are our adversaries,

in order that we no more have anything in common with these parasites and murderers of our Lord."[1]

Early Fathers of Christianity

Anti-Semitism in Christianity continued with the writings of the early church fathers, a poisonous stream of venom from the mouths of the supposed spiritual leaders. Christian hatred for the Jews, masked as spiritual teaching, reached a climax in the writings of St. John Chrysostom (A.D. 345–407), who was known as the Bishop with the Golden Mouth. The first in a long line of Christian leaders to label the Jews as "Christ killers," Chrysostom's Jew-hating sermons were classic Christian reading for centuries.

At Easter, the Christian clergy would enflame the passions of the faithful until the saints would race out of the church with clubs, run to the Jewish quarter, and beat Jews to death for what they did to Jesus on the cross. It became an annual custom at Easter to drag a Jew into the church and slap him on the face before the altar. "This ceremony was sometimes carried out with excessive vigor; on one occasion, recounts a monkish chronicler (without, however, expressing any disapproval), a distinguished nobleman who was taking the part of chief celebrant 'knocked out the eyes and the brains of the perfidious one (disbelieving Jew), who fell dead on the spot'...his brethren from the synagogue took the body out of the church and buried it."[2]

The Crusaders

The perfection of Christian hatred eventually gave birth to the **Dark Ages and the Crusades**. During the First Crusade to the Holy Land, in 1096, the crusading armies, called Knights of the Cross, left a trail of Jewish blood across Europe. Within a six-month period, some ten thousand Jews were slaughtered—up to one-third of the Jewish population of Germany and France.[3]

Some Jewish communities were given the opportunity to save their lives by meeting the Crusaders' demand for huge amounts of gold and silver. Those Jewish communities who could not meet the ransom demand were butchered in the name of God. Others said a final prayer and killed their wives and children mercifully and quickly, lest the cross-carrying Crusaders butcher them. Then fathers committed suicide to preserve the sanctity of the name of Jehovah God.

The Crusaders were not holy men on a holy mission. They were a mismatched and misled mob of thieves, murderers, and rapists who believed their sins had been forgiven in advance by the pope. In fact, not only could a Crusader consider his sins forgiven, but all his financial debts to any Jewish creditor were canceled as well. It is no wonder that so many adventurous young Europeans signed up for the cause. To them, it was a quick way to get out of debt, both in this life and, in theory, the next.

As a "bonus," the Crusaders were permitted to rob the Jews of their possessions. They could murder the Jews and rape their daughters and wives, and all was forgiven by the pope even before they left on the Crusade. Why? Because the Roman church, in an attempt to take control of Jerusalem, declared it was the will of God.

In 1099, Godfrey's Crusade was the first to reach Jerusalem, invading the city through the Jewish quarter. As the onslaught began, desperate Jews sought protection in the synagogue, locking the doors behind them. This attempt to save their lives proved futile. Upon discovering the locked synagogue crowded with Jews, the Crusaders set it on fire. They marched around the synagogue singing "Christ We Adore Thee," while from inside the building the horrified screams of 969 helpless men, women, and children begged for mercy as they were burned alive.[4] Afterward, all non-Christians were banned from living in Jerusalem.

Is it any wonder, then, that today the word *crusade* makes Jews nauseous? A Christian sees the cross and thinks of forgiveness of sin; a Jew looks at the cross and sees an electric chair, a sign of death—a sign under which his relatives have been slaughtered for two thousand years.

The Fourth Lateran Council

The Fourth Lateran Council met in November of 1215 in response to the call of Pope Innocent III. More than one thousand church delegates met in four stormy sessions to determine what the official relationship between Christians and Jews should be under Roman Catholic policy. One of the edicts that resulted from the Fourth Lateran Council was a formal declaration supporting the oppressive, violent conduct of the Roman church toward the Jews during prior centuries. It would be the officially approved standard of conduct for European Christians toward Jews through the centuries and was still in place when Adolf Hitler would eventually come to power.

The Council declared that all Jews must wear the badge of shame. Concerned that Christians and Jews would enter into sexual relationships, the church fathers forced the Jews to wear distinctive clothing so that they could be recognized on sight. "In order that the offence of such a damnable mixing may not spread further, under the excuse of a mistake of this kind, we decree that such persons of either sex, in every Christian province and at all times, are to be distinguished in public from other people by the character of their dress—seeing moreover that this was enjoined upon them by Moses himself, as we read."[5]

The reference to distinctive dress being enjoined by Moses refers to the fact that Moses instructed the men of Israel to make prayer shawls (Numbers 15:37–41) that were to be worn by all adult men from "generation to generation." The church fathers used Moses's description of a prayer shawl as scriptural justification to force all Jews of "both sexes in every Christian province" to dress distinctively, an obvious abuse of that scripture.

When Adolf Hitler came to power in the twentieth century, he was able to use this four-centuries-old edict to force the Jews to wear the "yellow badge," a Star of David emblem, thereby targeting them for abuse and execution. Hitler was able to easily segregate the Jewish citizens from the rest of the population by simply implementing long-standing church policy that visibly marked Jews.

The Fourth Lateran Council also ruled that Jews must tithe to the Roman church. The Jews were ordered to pay tithes (10 percent of their gross income) to the church because the Jews were now owners of lands that had previously belonged to Christians. The Roman church could not afford a loss of revenue just because a Christian had sold his property to a perfidious Jew, so they decided to recoup their losses by imposing a strict financial levy.

The exact reading of the council edict states: "We decree, under the same penalty, that Jews shall be compelled to make satisfaction to churches for tithes and offerings due to the churches, which the churches were accustomed to receive from Christians for houses and other possessions, before they passed by whatever title to the Jews, so that the churches may thus be preserved from loss."[6] This ecclesiastical edict was nothing short of extortion. It was economic control of the Jews using the law.

In this area too the Fourth Lateran Council was laying down church policy that would pave the way for Nazi political policy. On April 1, 1933, sixty days after Adolf Hitler had sworn before the German people to "conduct my affairs of office impartially and with justice to everyone," he declared a general boycott of every Jewish business in the Third Reich.[7] It was, yet again, economic control of the Jews through the law.

The Fourth Lateran Council also decreed that Jews could not hold public office and called upon the secular powers to "exterminate all heretics."[8]

On April 7, 1933, the German Third Reich passed a law with the pompous title, "Law for the Restoration of the Professional Civil Service." The lofty-sounding piece of legislation was the legal instrument through which the Nazis dismissed every Jew working in a civil service job in Germany. Overnight, thousands of Jews were without jobs. It was, once again, economic control of the Jews through the law and a reflection of a long-standing policy of the Catholic Church.

In each of these instances, Hitler, the most notable example of anti-Semitism in the twentieth century, simply enforced policies that had been approved by the church over the course of history and that remained the official policy of the church when the Nazi party came to power.

The Spanish Inquisition

The Spanish Inquisition began in 1481, striking the Jews like a bolt of lightning out of the blue heavens. For years the Jews of Spain were under extreme pressure to convert to the Roman church. Many did and were called *marranos* (pigs). They were hated by the Jews for being traitors to Judaism and hated by the church, which believed they were practicing Judaism secretly while pretending to be Catholics.

Religious fervor mounted until Ferdinand and Isabella appealed to Pope Sixtus IV in 1477 to establish an Inquisition. The point must be made that this Inquisition was established by the Roman church and received its power directly from the pope. Its purpose was to purge the church of heretics, particularly former Jews whose forced conversions to Christianity were in question.

Two Dominican monks, Miguel de Morillo and Juan de San Martin, were appointed to lead the Inquisition on September 27, 1480. The wealthy and notable personalities of the Jewish community were brought before the religious court. Joseph

Telushkin describes the period of the Inquisition this way: "Those people who refused to confess even after being convicted, or who were courageous enough to acknowledge that they were still Jews, were repeatedly tortured to force them to concede to the truth of Christianity. During the centuries in which the Inquisition had power, thousands of secret Jews were put on the rack, had water forced down their throats after their noses were pinched shut, or subjected to other tortures. All these actions were carried out by priests who claimed to be motivated only by love of the people they were torturing."[9] Hundreds were sentenced to be burned at the stake, and thousands returned to the church in terrified obedience.

The Inquisition was extended in October 1483, and under the fanatical leadership of Tomas de Torquemada, it reached levels of torture the Jews would not experience again until Hitler's sadistic Nazi SS Corps blossomed into its highest level of madness. Torquemada printed "Manuals of Inquisition," which gave hints on how to spot a "closet" Jew and how to extend and intensify the suffering of Jews on trial by flame, garrote, rack, whip, or needle. Inquisitional tortures continued from the late fifteenth century into the eighteenth century. During that time, 323,362 people were burned alive, and 17,659 were burned in effigy. It is one of the darkest periods of Spanish history.[10]

Martin Luther

Italy and Spain were not the only European nations to persecute the Jews throughout history. During the Dark Ages and the centuries that followed, Jews were robbed, tortured, and murdered across

England, France, and Germany. It would be Germany, however, that would produce two of the most powerful anti-Semitic influences of all time.

Few people have had greater influence on the Protestant faith than Martin Luther. Yet it was his anti-Semitism that was so deeply appreciated by Adolf Hitler. "The worst evil genius of Germany," wrote Dean Inge, "is not Hitler, or Bismarck, or Frederick the Great, but Martin Luther."[11]

Martin Luther triggered the Reformation when he nailed his Ninety-five Theses to the cathedral door. Early in his ministry, Luther was convinced the Jewish people would be delighted with his new brand of Christianity and would join in his assault on the Catholic Church. He made complimentary remarks about the Jewish contribution to Christianity. But when the Jews did not join Luther, he turned on them with a vulgarity and vengeance that would eventually provide many suitable texts for Hitler's program of extermination.

Some of the most vicious, Jew-hating statements ever made are found in his tract entitled "Concerning the Jews and Their Lies." It reads as follows:

> Let me give you my honest advice.
>
> First, their synagogues or churches should be set on fire, and whatever does not burn up should be covered or spread over with dirt so that no one may ever be able to see a cinder or stone of it. And this ought to be done for the honor of God and of Christianity in order that God may see that we are Christians...

Secondly, their homes should be broken down and destroyed.

Thirdly, they should be deprived of their prayer books and Talmuds in which such idolatry, lies, cursing and blasphemy are taught.

Fourthly, their rabbis must be forbidden under the threat of death to teach any more...

Fifthly, passport and traveling privileges should be absolutely forbidden the Jews. Let them stay at home.

Sixthly, they ought to be stopped from usury. For this reason, as said before, everything they possess they stole and robbed from us through their usury, for they have not other means of support.

Seventhly, let the young and strong Jews and Jewesses be given the flail, the ax, the hoe, the spade, the distaff, and spindle, and let them earn their bread by the sweat of their noses as is enjoined upon Adam's children. We ought to drive the lazy bones out of our system.

If, however, we are afraid that they might harm us personally, or our wives, children, servants, cattle, etc., then let us apply the same cleverness (expulsion) as the other nations, such as France, Spain, Bohemia, etc., and settle with them for that which they have extorted from us, and after having it divided up fairly let us drive them out of the country for all time.

To sum up, dear princes and nobles who have Jews in your domains, if this advice of mine does not suit you, then find a better one so that you and we may all be free from this insufferable devilish burden—the Jews.[12]

Those were some of the last words penned by Martin Luther. Four centuries later, however, his tract prescribing vicious treatment of the Jewish people would be carried out almost to the letter in his own country.

When the Nazis placed the Jews in ghetto stables and camps, they were following Luther's precepts; when they burned Jewish synagogues, homes, and schools, they were carrying out Luther's will; when the Germans robbed the Jews of their possessions, they were doing Luther's bidding; when the Germans reduced the Jews to concentration camp slavery, they merely followed the teaching of Luther to make the Hebrews slaves of the serfs!

While Adolf Hitler, a Catholic, was primarily motivated by notions of racial purity, he freely relied on Luther's theology in presenting his rationale to the German people. His Nazi murder machine showed "a proper appreciation of the continuity of their history when they declared that the first large-scale Nazi pogrom (violent physical persecution of Jews) in November 1938 was a pious operation performed in honor of the anniversary of Luther's birthday."[13]

Adolf Hitler and the Holocaust

Adolf Hitler's atrocities toward the Jews have been chronicled by the world's finest scholars. There is no purpose in retracing his bloody steps, which dragged Europe and the world into the bowels of hell for twelve years of an unspeakable nightmare.

What is pertinent to this text is to demonstrate how Roman church policy shaped the policy of the Third Reich. When Hitler signed a treaty with the Vatican in Rome, he said, "I am only continuing the work of the Catholic Church."[14] In this chapter I've included a comparison of the historical record of church policy and Nazi policy.[15]

Roman Church Policy	Nazi Policy
1. Prohibition of intermarriage and of sexual intercourse between Christians and Jews, Synod of Elvira, A.D. 306	1. Law for the Protection of German Blood and Honor, September 15, 1935 (RGB1 I, 1146)
2. Jews and Christians not permitted to eat together, Synod of Elvira, A.D. 306	2. Jews barred from dining cars, December 30, 1939, Document NG-3995
3. Jews not allowed to hold public office, Synod of Clermont, A.D. 535; also Fourth Lateran Council, A.D. 1215	3. Law for Re-Establishment of the Professional Civil Service, April 7, 1935 (RGB1 I, 175), in which Jews were expelled from office and their civil service jobs
4. Jews not allowed to employ Christian servants or possess Christian slaves, Third Synod of Orleans, A.D. 538	4. Law for the Protection of German Blood and Honor. September 15, 1935 (RGB1 I, 1146), forbade Germans from hiring Jews
5. Jews not permitted to show themselves in the streets during Passion Week, Third Synod of Orleans, A.D. 538	5. Decree authorizing local authorities to bar Jews from the streets on certain days (i.e., Nazi holidays), December 3, 1938 (RGB1 I, 1676)

Roman Church Policy	Nazi Policy
6. Burning of the Talmud and other books, Twelfth Synod of Toledo, A.D. 681	6. Nazi book burnings in Germany
7. Christians not permitted to patronize Jewish doctors, Trulanic Synod, A.D. 692	7. Decree of July 25, 1938 (RGB1 I, 969), forbidding Germans from patronizing Jewish doctors
8. Jews obligated to pay taxes for support of the church to the same extent as Christians, Fourth Lateran Council, A.D. 1215	8. Jews to pay a special tax for Nazi party purposes imposed on December 24, 1940 (RGB1 I, 1666)
9. Jews not permitted to be plaintiffs or witnesses against Christians in the courts, Third Lateran Council, A.D. 1179, Canon 26	9. Jews not permitted to institute civil suits, September 9, 1942 (NG-151)
10. Jews not permitted to withhold inheritance from descendants who had accepted Christianity, Third Lateran Council, A.D. 1179, Canon 26	10. Decree empowering the Justice Ministry to void wills offending the "sound judgment of the people," July 31, 1938 (RGB1 I, 937)
11. The marking of Jewish clothes with a badge, Fourth Lateran Council, A.D. 1215, Canon 68	11. Decree of September 1, 1941, forcing all Jews to wear the yellow Star of David (RGB1 I, 547)
12. Construction of new synagogues prohibited, Council of Oxford, A.D. 1222	12. Destruction of synagogues in entire Reich, November 10, 1938 (Heydrich to Goring PS-3058)

Roman Church Policy	Nazi Policy
13. Christians not permitted to attend Jewish ceremonies, Synod of Vienna, A.D. 1267	13. Friendly relations with Jews prohibited, October 24, 1941 (Gestapo directive, L-15)
14. Jews forced to live in ghettos away from Christians, Synod of Breslau, A.D. 1267	14. Jews forced to live in ghettos, Order of Heydrich, September 21, 1939 (PS-3363)
15. Jews not permitted to obtain academic degrees, Council of Basel, A.D. 1434, Session XIX	15. All Jews expelled from schools and universities throughout the Third Reich with the Law against Overcrowding of German schools and Universities, April 25, 1933 (RGB1 I, 225)
16. Mass extermination of the Jews in the Crusades. Fourth Lateran Council called upon secular powers to "exterminate all heretics," A.D. 1215. The Inquisitions burned them at the stake by the thousands while confiscating their property,	16. Hitler's "Final Solution" called for the systematic slaughter of every Jew in Europe. He took their homes, their jobs, their possessions (even their gold-filled teeth), their names, and finally their very lives. His justification? "It's the will of God" and "it's the work of the church."

The Holocaust did not begin with Hitler lining the Jews up for the gas chamber; it began with religious leaders sowing the seeds of hatred within their congregations toward the Jewish people. Hitler quoted the Bible, chapter and verse, to justify his attack upon the Jews.

When a German general was asked at the Nuremberg Trials

how six million people could be systematically murdered by a German people who were among the world's most advanced societies, he said, "I am of the opinion that when for years, for decades, the doctrine is preached that Jews are not even human, such an outcome is inevitable."[16]

Christians today have difficulty understanding why Jewish people think of Adolf Hitler as a Christian. It's quite simple. The Jews equate Adolf Hitler with being a Christian for the same reason most people think any well-known preacher is a Christian. Most preachers attend and graduate from a Christian school and give dynamic public testimonies that they are Christians. When they preach, they quote the Bible and announce that they are called of God to carry out his mission.

Adolf Hitler also attended a Christian school under the tutelage of Padre Bernard Groner. As a small boy, Hitler told a friend that it was his ardent desire to become a priest. After he had written *Mein Kampf,* a text of his political and personal philosophy that included his desire to exterminate the Jews, he gave public testimony that "I am now, as before, a Catholic and will always remain so."[17]

He gave his testimony in December of 1941 when he announced his decision to implement the Final Solution after the bombing of Pearl Harbor. He ordered that the "killings should be done as humanely as possible. This was in line with his conviction that he was observing God's injunction to cleanse the world of vermin. He carried within him the Catholic teaching that the Jew was the killer of God. The extermination, therefore, could be carried out without a twinge of conscience since he was merely acting as the avenging hand of God."[18]

One thousand years of Christian anti-Semitism came into full bloom, and in short order one-third of European Jews were choked to death on Zyklon B gas, a cyanide-based insecticide, or slaughtered in open pits, their nude bodies piled in heaps. At the Nuremberg Trials, the following testimony was given in answer to questions about what was done to Jewish children at the concentration camps:

> They killed them with their parents, in groups and alone. They killed them in children's homes and hospitals, burying them alive and in graves, throwing them into flames, stabbing them with bayonets, poisoning them, conducting experiments upon them, extracting their blood for the use of the German army, throwing them into prison and Gestapo torture chambers and concentration camps where the children died from hunger, torture, and epidemic diseases.[19]

> Very frequently women would hide their children under their clothes, but of course when we found them we would send the children in to be exterminated.[20]

> Mothers in the throes of childbirth shared cars with those infected with tuberculosis or venereal disease. Babies, when born, were hurled out of these cars' windows.[21]

> At that time, when the greatest number of Jews were exterminated in the gas chambers, an order was issued that the children were to be thrown into the crematory ovens, or into the crematory ditches, without previous asphyxiation

with gas....The children were thrown in alive, their cries could be heard all over the camp.[22]

If Jesus and his disciples had lived in Europe in 1940, they would have been prodded into cattle cars at bayonet point and shipped to Auschwitz. *Remember: they were all Jews!*

Arriving at Auschwitz, they would have been ushered into a gas chamber en masse to scratch and claw at the walls in terror as they frantically gasped for breath. Jesus Christ, along with Peter, James, John, and the rest, would have slowly choked to death on the poisonous gas for fifteen long minutes, still standing grotesquely erect because they were packed too tightly to fall.

It makes for an entirely different story when you see the Jewish people as the family of Jesus Christ. Hitler's propaganda machine separated Jesus from his Jewish heritage. In Hitler's writings, Jesus Christ was, in fact, the first Jew hater. "Christ was the greatest early fighter in the battle against the world enemy, the Jews," ranted Hitler.[23]

In America today many preachers still try to separate Jesus Christ from his Jewish heritage and the Jewish people, calling the Jews "our dilemma." They are trying to pit the church against God's chosen people by saying that the "church is the only true Israel."

And yet, there are glimmers of hope.

The Reconciliation Begins...

Pope John Paul II will be remembered for many of the worthwhile causes he supported, but for the Jewish people, the most important elements of John Paul's work involved reconciling the Roman Catholic Church with its anti-Semitic past, memorializing the Holocaust, and officially recognizing the State of Israel. Some have said he will be remembered as "the best pope the Jews ever had."[24]

John Paul's successor, Pope Benedict XVI, has assured Jewish leaders that the Roman Catholic Church is committed to fighting anti-Semitism and to forging closer ties between Jews and Catholics.

My own desire for reconciliation with my Jewish brothers and sisters—who worship the God of Abraham, Isaac, and Jacob as I do—began on my first trip to Israel in 1978, and it deepened as I contemplated the long history of Christian atrocities against the Jewish people. In 1981 that desire for reconciliation turned into a personal reality. I became friends with a local rabbi in San Antonio. And friends can bridge the greatest of chasms.

CHAPTER 4

"ONE SINGLE NIGHT" BECOMES MANY

WHILE I WAS DELVING INTO THE HISTORY OF THE persecution of the Jewish people, I was also studying the Jewish roots of Christianity. I preached a sermon on the symbolism of the *tallit*, the prayer shawl I had bought in Jerusalem, showing how it was the garment touched by the sick woman in Luke 9. She was cured of more than a decade of hemorrhaging when she touched the tassels on the hem of Jesus's prayer shawl. Such healings, I discovered, were the fulfillment of a prophecy in Malachi: "the Sun of Righteousness shall arise with healing in His wings" (Malachi 4:2). The word translated *wings* refers to the tassels on a *tallit*.

Still, I had done nothing to follow up on the pledge I'd made to do something to bring Jews and Christians together. After we returned from our trip to Israel, I discovered that a member of our tour group had taken a photo of me praying at the Western Wall, and the photo also captured the elderly man who was wearing the prayer shawl while reciting the Torah. I had the photo enlarged and hung it in my office as a reminder of the powerful experience I'd had that day in Jerusalem.

My days were consumed with pastoring a growing church, and Diana and I were busy raising a growing family. Like my father, I was a voracious reader and kept up with news about Israel and the Middle East, but it was not an all-consuming passion for me.

That changed on the first Sunday in June 1981, when I got caught up in the media storm that erupted over the Israeli bombing of Iraq's nuclear reactor, which intelligence had indicated was being used by Saddam Hussein in pursuit of nuclear weapons.

In the 1970s, Iraq's dictator had persuaded the French government to assist in the building of an Osiris-class nuclear materials test reactor and production laboratory. The French, who also supplied Iraq with a substantial amount of highly enriched uranium fuel, dubbed the facility *Osirak* after its nuclear classification, Osiris (the Egyptian god of the dead), and the country, Iraq. The Iraqis, however, called the reactor *Tammuz 1,* in honor of the month during which Saddam Hussein's Ba'ath party took over the reigns of government in 1968.

During the late 1970s, a number of Western governments were concerned that Iraq was preparing to use the reactor for weapons-grade plutonium production. Israel was especially concerned and pursued diplomatic relations with France, Italy (from whom the Iraqi government had previously tried to purchase a reactor), and the United States. But with no assurance that production would be halted, and with the French government continuing to assist Iraq's nuclear program, the Israeli government decided to take action *before* the reactor was loaded with nuclear fuel. Once that happened, it would be impossible to eliminate Osirak without a high risk of radioactive fallout, which would have the potential of harming not just the Iraqi population but also the people of surrounding countries. (The 1986 explosion of the Chernobyl reactor in Ukraine demonstrated just how devastating such radioactive fallout could be.)

Shortly after the commencement of the Iran-Iraq war in 1980, Iranian forces attacked the Osirak reactor during an air raid on September 30. The damage, however, was not serious enough to stop Saddam Hussein's nuclear program. Therefore, on Sunday, June 7, 1981, Israel's air force finished the job Iran had started nine months earlier. Called Operation Opera, the Israeli mission was led by a squadron of eight F-16 multipurpose fighter jets escorted by six F-15 tactical fighters. The heavily fueled aircraft flew 680 miles— undetected over Saudi and Jordanian airspace—to reach their target. In a surgical strike the eight F-16s released their weapons, and all sixteen Mark 84 bombs hit the Osirak reactor.

With Osirak incapacitated, Saddam Hussein's nuclear plans were derailed, at least for the time being. Israel, as well as the rest of the Middle East, was safe.

But the political fallout against Israel was swift and loud. In the days following the June 1981 preemptive strike, I grew increasingly frustrated by the one-sided media coverage. One evening, I had had all of it I could take. I was sitting in an overstuffed chair in my den, newspaper in my lap, feet propped up on the ottoman. The print media was blasting Israel on page after page, so I tossed the newspaper aside and turned on the television news. Same story. All three networks featured footage from stern-faced reporters standing outside the United Nations, where the Security Council was threatening to pass a resolution condemning Israel. U.S. officials were joining the chorus of voices castigating Israel for taking action against the threat of nuclear devastation by a dictator who would think nothing of destroying the nation of Israel, even if it meant wiping out a sizable portion of Iraq's neighbors and allies.

Suddenly it was more than I could bear, and I found myself talking back to the television. "You're reading it all wrong," I yelled. "Israel has done the world a favor. They've taken nuclear weapons away from a madman, and all you mental midgets can do is beat up on them!"

After a minute I flicked off the TV and quit muttering. I picked up a legal pad and took it into the dining room so I could write at the table. A plan of action was forming in my mind: our church would put together a citywide night to *honor* Israel, not berate the beleaguered nation. For one single night, Israel would be the star. We would *celebrate* Israel.

My pen raced over the page as I jotted down ideas:

1. Have our choir sing Hebrew songs.
2. Take crew to record the event and air on national TV program.
3. Contact all the pastors in San Antonio; make it a citywide event.
4. Book the Lila Cockrell Theater downtown.
5. Invite local rabbis and leaders in the Jewish community to attend.

Diana walked into the room and asked what I was doing. "We're going to have a citywide event to honor Israel," I said, and I started reading the items on my list to her.

When I finished reading my list, Diana said, "Don't you think you should contact some people in the Jewish community before you start writing all the pastors and making all those arrangements? What if they don't want to participate? Do you even know any rabbis?"

She might as well have thrown ice water in my face. I'd been on a roll with my grandiose plans. But before I could protest, I realized how practical her suggestion was. So I bumped the last item on my list up to the top, and I set about enlisting the participation of the Jewish leaders in San Antonio in what I had decided to call "A Night to Honor Israel."

In my naïveté, I had thought that would be the easiest step— how could they possibly *not* want to be a part of an event where people would be applauding the nation of Israel and where Jews and Christians could come together to acknowledge the things we had in common rather than the differences that pulled us apart?

It turned out, however, to be the most difficult step.

I started by paying a visit to the office of the Jewish Federation—without an appointment. I walked in unannounced and started talking about my plans to have A Night to Honor Israel.

The receptionist looked at me as if I had a bad rash that signaled some horrific disease. She had me repeat the information, and then she started asking questions.

"Who's going to be doing this?" she asked. I told her that Cornerstone Church would sponsor the event.

"And who will be participating with you?" She was taking notes as I talked.

"I'll be inviting all the pastors in town."

She finally looked up and said, "We'll need to have a committee meeting about that." Then she flipped pages on her desktop calendar and penciled in my name. "I'll let the local rabbis and community leaders know."

I went home with a date and time for a meeting. "I think they're like the Baptists," I joked with Diana later. "They do everything by committee."

I felt sure the committee meeting would be just a formality, so I started working with our music director and television producer on ideas for the event. But I held off writing the invitation letter to my fellow pastors in San Antonio. Good thing I did.

One committee meeting led to a second, which led to a third, and finally, to a fourth meeting, which went into the late hours of the night. The leaders of the Jewish community simply did not know what to make of me and my idea for A Night to Honor Israel. The debate was vocal and sometimes heated. It was a first for them—an evangelical pastor wanting to put together an event to honor the Jewish community and to raise money for a Jewish charity.

Finally, when it seemed that the fourth committee meeting would result in yet another impasse, Rabbi Aryeh Scheinberg stood up. I had met him once, a few months before, at an interfaith service held at Trinity Baptist Church. It had been just a casual introduction and a handshake, so I really didn't know anything about him other than that he was at least open to some kind of dialogue with Christians.

"Look," he said. "As Jews we know how to handle our enemies." He gestured with his palms turned upward. "But what if this man is a friend?"

It was like turning on a light in a dark room. The whole atmosphere changed. People began to relax, and soon there was a consensus: "OK, let's try it."

I can tell you now that without the courage of Aryeh Scheinberg, the first Night to Honor Israel would never have been held. Rabbi Scheinberg was, and is, the most respected rabbi in our city. His willingness to acknowledge that I just might be a friend was what it took for the Jewish Federation to be able to attend an event that I was, by this time, absolutely determined would take place.

With the Jewish community agreeing to participate, albeit with many concerns and reservations, I finally sat down and wrote my invitation to pastors in the San Antonio area. While the Jewish community hadn't quite known what to do with me, the Christian community did not have that problem. They knew exactly what they thought about the event, and it wasn't nice. Out of 150 invitations to pastors, I got a single positive response—from the esteemed Baptist pastor Dr. Buckner Fanning. He was the Billy Graham of San Antonio, a gracious and much-loved figure who had hosted the interfaith service at his church, Trinity Baptist, where I had briefly met Rabbi Scheinberg.

With Dr. Fanning and Rabbi Scheinberg enlisted in the cause, I called a press conference to let the entire city know about the upcoming event. The story made banner headlines. Within an hour after the newspaper hit the street, I received a death threat; it said that I would be shot before the event could even happen.

I took such threats seriously, so we hired private security for the Israel event. About ten years earlier a psychologically disturbed man had opened fire in our church one night while I was preaching. He shot directly at me from a distance of eight feet, emptying his revolver. Fortunately, I was not hit, and our ushers were able to subdue him. But having someone walk into my church with the intent of killing me had made a definite impression on me.

On Thursday, September 10, 1981—three months after I'd gotten fed up with the media attacks on Israel and determined to do something about it—I stood shoulder to shoulder with Dr. Fanning, Rabbi Scheinberg, and two other local rabbis on the stage of the Lila Cockrell Theater in downtown San Antonio. We made an unlikely team. Rabbi Scheinberg is about my height and build, but the similarities stop there. An Orthodox Jew, he has a full beard and always wears a yarmulke. As usual, *tzitzit*—the long white fringes at the four corners of the *tallit katan*, or small prayer shawl—hung visibly below his suit coat. By contrast, Dr. Fanning is slight of build, with a full head of wavy hair and the bearing of a senior statesman.

The 3,500-seat hall was filled, and I was thrilled to see the turnout from the Jewish community. All those committee meetings had finally paid off! Still, the tension in the air was thick enough to mute conversation as the people took their seats and Cornerstone's 120-voice choir and 40-piece orchestra took their positions on the stage.

The tension melted away to the sounds of Hebrew music, and the audience began to clap, sing, and enjoy themselves. I gave a speech stating why Christians should support Israel, and we took an offering and raised more than ten thousand dollars for Hadassah Hospital on the spot.

As Rabbi Scheinberg stood to give the benediction, the Director of Security slipped up beside me. He whispered in my ear that the *San Antonio Light*, a local newspaper, had just called the theater to alert us about a bomb threat on the building. According to the newspaper, the Lila Cockrell Theater was supposed to blow up at exactly 9:30 p.m.

I looked at my watch. It was 9:25.

As the rabbi prayed a blessing, I said an unspoken prayer of my own. "Lord, don't let him pray like Moses right now. Please let him pray like a Presbyterian late for lunch!"

When he finished the short benediction, we asked the crowd to disperse quickly. There was no bomb that night, but there was an explosion. It happened in our hearts. We had just been a part of something that was near the heart of God the Father, even though there were people who hated what we were doing.

What I had originally thought would be "one single night" to honor Israel turned into many such nights. Before long we had taken A Night to Honor Israel on the road, hosting and filming similar events in Dallas, Houston, Corpus Christi, Fort Worth, and Phoenix, Arizona. We took our choir and orchestra to Israel for A Night to Honor Israel tour. For the next twenty-five years we continued to hold these events, broadcasting them over national television for America to see.

During the Persian Gulf War in 1991, when Israel was repeatedly attacked by Iraqi Scud missiles, some of those in government who had so vehemently condemned Israel's attack on the Osirak reactor ten years earlier admitted, at least privately, that they were grateful for the preemptive strike that had destroyed it. And then on September 11, 2001—twenty years and one day after our first Night to Honor Israel—Americans' lives were changed forever. For the first time many Americans began to comprehend the threat of terror that the nation of Israel has lived with throughout its existence.

In February 2006 I decided the time had come to create a national grassroots movement focused on support for Israel. I called upon the foremost evangelical leaders from across America to join me in launching this new initiative. The reception I received this time was a far cry from the time I sent out 150 invitations to local pastors and received only one positive response. Every leader enthusiastically agreed to come to San Antonio to form a new group. I set forth an unbendable ground rule: members had to agree to set aside both theological and political agendas and focus on a single issue—support for Israel. We agreed that all Night to Honor Israel events would be nonconversionary.

My vision for this movement remains singular: to demonstrate Christian support for the State of Israel, and in so doing, to make the necessity of such support apparent to our local, state, and national officials.

More than four hundred Christian leaders—each with his or her own megachurch, television ministry, or publishing company—answered my call, and Christians United for Israel (CUFI) was born. Within a few short months, CUFI emerged as one of the most important Christian grassroots organizations in America. In July 2006, just five months from the time I began to reach out to pastors and parachurch organizations, we rallied more than 3,600 constituents to Washington DC for the first CUFI summit. We held a national Night to Honor Israel, and the following day we helped those 3,600 attendees meet with congressional leaders from their home state.

In July 2007, about forty-five hundred delegates from every state in the Union gathered in Washington DC for the second CUFI summit. Once again we charged up Capitol Hill to see our elected representatives, stating that the evangelical Christians of America were there to express solidarity with the State of Israel and the Jewish people around the world.

More and more evangelicals in America are becoming aware of the anti-Semitic teaching of the church toward the Jewish people, and they are denouncing it. As they develop a deep love for Israel and the Jewish people, millions of these Christians want to stand with them during these difficult days. Until recently, this Christian affection for the Jews had little influence in Washington. We're seeing that change rapidly and dramatically as evangelicals and Jews stand together to focus on the specific issue of Israel and the threats to Judeo-Christian civilization from radical Islam.

Before we can fully understand the depth of the threat radical Islam poses to our very way of life, we need to put this geopolitical issue in its historical and theological context. Where did these terrorist jihadist groups come from? Why does the Middle East seem to be a perpetual tinderbox ready to explode in violence and soak the ground with Jewish blood?

Let's take a look at the record. We start with the question, who are the Jews?

CHAPTER 5

THE PEOPLES OF
THE MIDDLE EAST

YOU CANNOT UNDERSTAND CURRENT AFFAIRS IN THE Middle East outside of the region's historical context. And you cannot understand the Arab-Israeli conflict without a clear view of the people who make up these two groups. We begin with this question: Who is a Jew?

It's an important question because the modern State of Israel offers the right of return to any Jewish person in the world. Exactly what is it that makes a person Jewish? Is it a genealogy tracing back to Abraham or a devout adherence to the Torah?

Modern-day Orthodox Jews recognize several criteria as sufficient to qualify a person as Jewish. A person need only meet one of the following criteria to be considered a Jew. Let's quickly examine each one:

- **Jewish mother.** This view acknowledges Jewish identity as being passed from mother to child. Bloodline, not faith, is the key consideration.

- **Belief in God and the Torah.** This view accords Jewish identity to those who have faith in Jehovah God as related in the Torah. This view allows Gentile conversion to Judaism.

- **Cultural tradition.** This view acknowledges those who practice Jewish customs and maintain Jewish traditions. This is the predominant view among American Jews, most of whom would be classified as Reform.

- **Personal choice/conversion.** This view acknowledges Jewish identity in anyone who undergoes conversion to Judaism because they have personally chosen to do so.

- **Ethnicity.** This view considers the primary element of Jewish identity to be ancestry of both parents. Homeland and religious faith and practice are also taken into consideration but are not required.

With so many different views on the definition of being Jewish, it's no wonder that confusion and controversy have surrounded the topic for centuries. Indeed, no controversy has been as heated or as long-lasting as this one. That's why, as Christians, we must rely on the words of the Bible as our plumb line for defining the identity of the Jewish people. The apostle Paul refers to God's position on the Jews and Israel in chapters 9 through 11 of the Book of Romans. As Paul begins his letter to the church at Rome, he writes:

For they are not all Israel who are of Israel.

—Romans 9:6

In St. Paul's teaching, Israel is a matter of election rather than birth (Romans 9:6–13). Not all those called "children of Abraham" (natural descendants) are actually his "seed" as demonstrated in Genesis 21:12, which states, "In Isaac your seed shall be called."

Remember that Abraham had two sons. His first son was Ishmael, born to the Egyptian maid Hagar. (See Genesis 16.) But, says Paul, Ishmael, though a physical descendant of Abraham, was not of the "seed" that produced Isaac, the spiritual child.

Ishmael was produced when Abraham was able to have children in his own sexual strength. Isaac was born by a supernatural act of God, since both Abraham and Sarah were well past the age of childbirth.

In Romans 9:8, Paul shifts from "children of the flesh" (Abraham) to "children of God." The shift is subtle but very significant. If Abraham's spiritual seed comes through God's promise and power, the Jewish people are not simply Abraham's seed but quite literally *God's children.*

This leads us into what is known as the doctrine of divine election, which is without a doubt the most controversial concept in Scripture. It is far more complex than I have room to address here.[1]

The divine codicil

Let's return to the mystery of Israel as explained by Paul in Romans 9–11. In order to understand this portion of Scripture, it is important that we first understand that these three chapters have no connection to the preceding or succeeding text in the Book of Romans. These three chapters are a *codicil*, a complete work within themselves. They stand alone, completely unique in their theme, which represents God's post-Calvary position paper on the Jewish people. This codicil was written by Paul to the Christians in Rome to explain God's position on the Jewish people and his plan whereby "all Israel will be saved" (Romans 11:26).

Some pastors teach that Romans 9–11 refers to the church, that the church has become a "spiritual Israel" and has replaced the Jewish people. This is an anti-Semitic theology that refuses to believe that God still has a place in his heart for Israel and the Jewish people. The prophet Zechariah clearly refers to the Jewish people as "the apple" (or pupil) of God's eye.

Other Bible teachers or preachers simply avoid Romans 9–11 because of the uncomfortable direction in which these complex verses pull us. But *ignoring* Scripture is not the same as *interpreting* Scripture.

After many years of study, I choose to interpret Romans 9, 10, and 11 as a stand-alone theological document. I have looked at this in greater detail in other writings, but I would like to briefly list for you now eight scriptural evidences to support my viewpoint.

Eight Biblical Evidences of National Israel

Evidence that Paul is outlining God's position on national Israel and not spiritual Israel (the church) is supported by his eight introductory statements that could *only* apply to the Jewish people as a *nation*.

> Who are Israelites, to whom pertain the adoption, the
> glory, the covenants, the giving of the law, the service of
> God, and the promises; of whom are the fathers and from
> whom, according to the flesh, Christ came...
>
> —Romans 9:4–5

1. The children of God

Israel is always represented in Scripture as God's children among all people (Deuteronomy 14:1; Hosea 11:1). When Paul talks about "the adoption" in Romans 9:4, he is referring to God's relationship with his firstborn (Exodus 4:22), the nation of Israel, not the church. Simply stated, there is no way the integrity of God would permit him to disinherit his firstborn son, national Israel, for spiritual Israel (the church).

2. The presence of God

In Romans 9:4, the glory Paul is talking about is *the Shekinah glory* or the visible presence of God (Ezekiel 1:28). This glory was visible as the luminous cloud that led Israel out of Egypt's bondage (Exodus 24:16) and the unmentionable presence that rested over the mercy seat in the holy of holies (Hebrews 9:5). It is the visible manifestation of God's presence with His chosen people.

3. The covenants with God

God gave the Jewish people the land of Israel by divine covenant. (See Genesis 15:17–21; 17:7–8). That covenant is a blood covenant; it is eternal and unbreakable. It cannot be amended by the United Nations or by the U.S. State Department. Any nation that forces Israel to "divide the land" will come under the swift and certain judgment of God (Joel 3:2).

The covenants God makes with his people are everlasting, without end. These covenants are not based on man's faithfulness to God; they are based on God's faithfulness to man. Those who teach that God has broken covenant with the Jewish people teach a false doctrine based on scriptural ignorance and a narcissistic attitude. If God broke covenant with the Jewish people, what scriptural justification do Christians have that he will not break covenant with us? The God of the Bible does not break covenant.

4. The law of God

The nation of Israel received the Torah or the written law of God, which was given to Moses on Mt. Sinai. The Torah was given to the Jewish people thousands of years before the Gentiles knew it existed (Romans 3:1–2).

Christians interpret Paul's rejection of the law for its powerlessness as rejection of its contents. However, Jesus said, "Do not think that I came to destroy the Law or the Prophets. I did not come to destroy but to fulfill" (Matthew 5:17).

5. The service of God

The service of God refers to the elaborate set of regulations for construction of the temple as well as the exact sacrificial system that would cleanse Israel from sin. For fifteen hundred years, the Jews—national Israel—were the only people who possessed this unique form of worship designed and commanded by God himself.

It was given to Moses at the top of Mount Sinai, where he received the Ten Commandments and all the Torah.

6. The promises of God

The Old Testament is full of many kinds of promises, but the promises Paul mentions in Romans 9:4 refer to the Messianic promises given to national Israel (not spiritual Israel) that a "Deliverer would come out of Zion" (Romans 11:26). However much the nations rejoice in the riches they have found in Jesus Christ, they must never forget that they were first promised to Israel and through national Israel they have come—not the church.

7. The patriarchs of God

The patriarchs are Abraham, Isaac, and Jacob, founders of the nation of Israel. In Romans 11:27–28, Paul makes this stunning statement: "'For this is My covenant with them [the Jewish people], when I shall take away their sins.'...They [the Jewish people] are beloved for the sake of the fathers." In this verse, "the fathers" refers to the patriarchs. The Jewish people are *permanently loved by God* because he made promises to Abraham, Isaac, and Jacob concerning the future of Israel and the Jewish people.

8. The Son of God

The Jewish people are the source of Jesus Christ. Jesus of Nazareth was born to a Jewish mother. He was a Jew among Jews. When Jesus spoke in the synagogue, only those who spoke Hebrew (the Jews) could listen. When He sent out apostles, only Jews were selected. When Rome crucified him at Golgotha and he gave up his soul, a sign hung over his head that read: "This is the king of the Jews."

These eight evidences as recorded by the apostle Paul verify beyond any reasonable doubt that the message of Romans 9–11 is God's position regarding national Israel and is intended exclusively for the Jewish people.

Today there are some thirteen to fourteen million Jews worldwide. About half of them reside in North and South America, while 37 percent reside in Israel.[2] Tel Aviv is home to 2.5 million Jews, making it the city with the largest Jewish population in the world. It is followed by New York City (1.9 million), Haifa (655,000), Los Angeles (621,000), and Jerusalem (570,000).[3]

Jewish people are commonly divided into two groups: Ashkenazic and Sephardic Jews. *Ashkenaz* is Hebrew for Germany, and *Sefarad* is Hebrew for Spain. Jews whose families come from Europe and speak Yiddish are regarded as Ashkenazim, and those whose families come from Spain or the Arab world are called Sephardim.

Other People in the Middle East

Now that we've learned more about who the Jewish people are, let's turn to the other peoples of the Middle East.

The Arabs

The word *Arab* can be used historically to refer to the people who originated from the Arabian Peninsula or ethnically to all the various people who speak the Arabic language. It typically refers to the natives of the following countries: Algeria, Bahrain, Egypt,

Iraq, Jordan, Kuwait, Lebanon, Libya, Morocco, Oman, Qatar, Saudi Arabia, Sudan, Syria, Tunisia, the United Arab Emirates, and Yemen. Palestinians, although not from an independent country, are also included in this ethnic group.

The overwhelming majority of Arabs are Muslims, with most of them being Sunni Muslims. The remaining members of the population in these countries are Christians and Jews, commonly viewed by other Arabs as infidels. In many places these minorities have only two choices: convert or be killed.

There are Arabs living in Israel, the West Bank, and the Gaza Strip as well.

The Berbers

The Berbers are an indigenous people of Northwest Africa. Most North African Arabs have Berber ancestry. The word *Berber* does not exist in their language; they identify themselves using the word *Imazighen* in their native tongue.

There are about 72 million Berbers living in Algeria, Libya, and Morocco. Most Berbers are Sunni Muslims (99 percent). Before the introduction of Islam, most Berbers were Christians. Judaism was also present in some regions.[4]

The Kurds

The Kurds are an ethnic group of unknown origin who consider themselves indigenous to the Kurdistan region, which encompasses adjacent portions of Iran, Iraq, Syria, and Turkey. They are closely related to Iranians and speak Kurdish, an Indo-European language.

The majority of Kurds are Sunni Muslims, but it has been said that Kurds "hold their Islam lightly," meaning that they are not as impassioned by their faith as other Muslims can be.

The CIA *World Factbook* reports that roughly 54 percent of the world's Kurds live in Turkey, 19 percent in Iran, 21 percent in Iraq, and slightly more than 6 percent in Syria. In all of these countries, Kurds form the second largest people group. These estimates place the total number of Kurds at somewhere between 25 and 36 million.[5]

The Palestinians

There are approximately 9.6 million people who identify themselves as Palestinians worldwide.[6] In Israel the majority of them live in the Gaza Strip and in the area referred to by the media as the West Bank. The overwhelming majority of Palestinians are Sunni Muslims; however, there are some Palestinian Jews and Christians.

I want to clear up some misconceptions about who the Palestinians are and their claim on the land of Israel. The land of Israel has never belonged to Palestinians. Never! It was labeled Palaestina by the Roman emperor Hadrian in A.D. 130, but there has never been a land called Palestine. There is no Palestinian language. Before 1948, the people now called Palestinians lived in Egypt. They lived in Syria. They lived in Iraq. They moved into the land of Israel when they were displaced by the war of 1948, which the Arab nations started, but Israel is not occupying territory these people now call home. Referring to Israel as "occupied territory" is propaganda. Israel abandoned the Gaza Strip in an effort to achieve peace, but it backfired. Gaza is now the foundation of a terrorist state headed by the Hamas terrorist organization, which is sworn to Israel's destruction.

The Pashtuns

Pashtuns are ethnic Afghans who make up the largest people group in Afghanistan and the second largest group in Pakistan. They speak the Pashto language and adhere to *Pashtunwali* (a religious code of honor) and Islam. There are approximately 13 million Pashtuns living in Afghanistan and 25 million in Pakistan. A little more than 80 percent of the refugees living in Pakistan are Pashtuns from neighboring Afghanistan.[7]

The *Taliban* (meaning "students" or "seekers of knowledge") is a Sunni Muslim movement that ruled most of Afghanistan from 1996 until 2001; it currently fights against foreign forces within Afghanistan. The majority of Taliban members are Pashtun.[8]

The Persians

Persians are the main ethnic group of Iran, with approximately 35 million Persians making up 51 percent of the population. They also inhabit neighboring countries such as Afghanistan, Tajikistan, and Uzbekistan. Most Iranians are Shia Muslims (89 percent). Some are Sunni Muslims (9 percent). Zoroastrians, Christians, Jews, atheists, and agnostics combine for the remaining 2 percent.[9]

Iran was known as Persia until 1935 and became an Islamic republic when the shah was overthrown and sent into exile in 1979.

The Turks

Historically, the word *Turk* or *Turkish* was used to refer to all Muslim inhabitants of the Ottoman Empire regardless of their ethnicity. Today, the word is primarily used to refer to the inhabitants of Turkey. Modern-day Turkey has a population of 70 million and is made up of two main ethnic groups: Turks (80 percent) and Kurds (20 percent). The vast majority of Turks are Sunni Muslims (99.8 percent).[10]

As we identified the various people groups in the Middle East, it probably became quite clear to you that Islam is the prevalent religion. But how does Islam differ from Judaism and Christianity? Let's examine the evidence.

CHAPTER 6

THE RELIGIONS OF THE MIDDLE EAST

J UDAISM, CHRISTIANITY, AND ISLAM ARE OFTEN REFERRED TO as the major monotheistic religions; that is, they all teach that there is one God. Further, they all had their origins in the area we call today the Middle East.

A fourth monotheistic religion, *Zoroastrianism*, comes from ancient Persia, which is modern Iran. This faith is based on the teachings of the prophet Zoroaster, who proclaimed that Ahura Mazda is the one transcendent God, creator of the universe. Another older name for this faith is Mazdaism. While once prevalent, this religion has waned in importance in the Middle East, and the number of modern adherents has dwindled to a few hundred thousand. Most people in Iran today are Muslims.

Because America is, despite how secularists portray it, a Judeo-Christian nation, the basic tenets of these faiths are familiar enough that I will not detail them here. For our purposes it is important to remember, as I have said before, that both Jews and

Christians worship the same God, the God of Abraham, Isaac, and Jacob. These are the historic roots of both faiths. Judaism does not need Christianity to explain its existence while Christianity cannot define its existence without Judaism.

That leads us to Islam, whose followers are called Muslims. They also believe in one supreme being, who is called Allah. But is Allah the same divine authority worshiped by Jews and Christians? Quite simply, no.

Allah

The name *Allah* comes from an Arabic term expressing the concept of a supreme god, al-Ilah (the deity). Prior to Muhammad, Arabs worshiped many gods and goddesses, and the origins of Islam derive from worship of the moon god of Mecca in pre-Islamic Arabia. According to George Braswell, "Contemporary Islam also focuses on the moon, indicated by a crescent atop the mosque, a lunar calendar, and with festivals like Ramadan regulated by the rising of the moon."[1]

The Allah described in the Quran, the scriptures sacred to Muslims, is not the same as the God of Abraham, Isaac, and Jacob revealed in the Bible. Don't be deceived by those who would try to convince you otherwise. The god of Islam is totally different from the God of the Bible.

For starters, Allah is unapproachable, and unknowable, whereas the Bible tells us that God desires to know us and have an ongoing relationship with us. The Quran teaches that Allah works with Satan and demons to lead people astray in order to populate the hell he created (Surah 6:39, 126; 32:13; 43:36–37). By contrast, our Father God loves the people of the world so much "that He gave His only begotten Son, that whoever believes in Him should not perish but have everlasting life" (John 3:16).[2]

Allah Contrasted With Jehovah[3]	
Muslims Believe…	**Christians and Jews Believe…**
Allah revealed his will.	Jehovah revealed himself.
Allah is removed from his creation; he relates to them through his will and law.	Jehovah created humans for fellowship; he relates to them personally and experientially.
Doctrine of singularity: God is neither plural nor triune.	Christians hold to the doctrine of the triune God: Father, Son, and Holy Spirit.
Allah is impersonal.	God is love.
The Quran teaches that Allah cannot be called Father; he has no son, no daughter, no parents.	The Bible teaches that Jehovah is our heavenly Father; believers are called his sons and daughters.
Allah made a covenant with Abraham to give the Promised Land to the descendants of Ishmael.	Jehovah made a covenant with Abraham to give the Promised Land to Isaac and his descendants.
Jesus was created from the dust, like Adam.	Christians believe that Jesus was conceived by the Holy Spirit and born of a virgin.

Allah Contrasted With Jehovah[3]	
Muslims Believe...	**Christians and Jews Believe...**
Jesus did not die on the cross.	Christians teach that Jesus died on the cross for the remission of our sins.
In a messiah called the Mahdi.	Christians believe that Jesus is the Messiah; Jews believe the Messiah is yet to be revealed.
The messiah will be a descendant of Muhammad.	Christians and Jews believe the Messiah will be a descendant of King David.
The messiah will conquer Israel.	Most Christians and Jews believe the Messiah will rescue Israel.

The Prophet Muhammad

Muhammad, the founder of the religion of Islam, is considered by Muslims to be "the last prophet of God." Muhammad was born in Mecca, Arabia, in A.D. 570. His father died before he was born, and his mother died when he was six years old. He was raised by his paternal grandfather, worked as a merchant, and married a wealthy caravan owner named Khadija by age twenty-six. Khadija was forty years old and had been divorced four times when she proposed to Muhammad, but this did not stop the two from marrying and having six children together.

Muhammad's first "revelation" from Allah occurred in a mountain cave outside of Mecca when he was forty years old. A few years later, he began preaching about his revelations, proclaiming that he was a prophet and messenger of God along the same line as Noah, Abraham, Moses, and Jesus, and that "surrender" (*Islam*) to Allah is man's religion. The revelations Muhammad received from Allah throughout his life form the verses of the Quran, which Muslims regard as the divine word of God.

His first converts to Islam were his wife, Khadija, and his ten-year-old cousin; Muhammad had few followers early on. To escape persecution, he eventually migrated to Medina with his lonely band of followers. He was then able to unite two warring tribes and convert them to Islam. He spent the next eight years battling the tribes of Mecca. Meanwhile, he sent out twelve key followers to spread the message of Islam on his behalf, and by the time he conquered Mecca, his following had grown to ten thousand people. At the time of his death in A.D. 632, most of Arabia had converted to Islam.

Muhammad slaughtered thousands of people in establishing and spreading Islam. He told his followers, "Who relinquishes his faith, kill him....I have been ordered by Allah to fight with people till they testify there is no god but Allah, and Muhammad is his messenger."[4]

After this quote from Muhammad, you may be asking yourself: What exactly do modern-day Muslims really believe? To answer that question, first allow me to give you a brief description of the two main branches of Islam—Sunni and Shia—divided by who they believe Muhammad's rightful successors to be.

Sunni Islam

Sunni Muslims comprise approximately 90 percent of the Islamic world. Adherents to the Sunni branch of Islam believe that all of Muhammad's successors—the first four caliphs and their heirs, who ruled the Muslim world until the end of World War I—are the rightful leaders of Muslims. They believe that Muhammad intentionally refrained from appointing a successor before he died so that his teachings in the Quran could stand alone as guidance for all Muslims. Caliphs and other religious leaders are appointed by a consensus of the people and do not carry spiritual authority. Therefore, in the Sunni branch of Islam, an imam (an Arabic word meaning "leader") is simply a religious leader or teacher of Islam.

Shia Islam

Followers of Shia Islam—called Shiites—make up only 10 percent of the Muslim population. Shiites are concentrated in Iran, Iraq, and Lebanon. Followers of the Shia branch of Islam believe that only the descendants of the fourth caliph, Ali, are the legitimate successors of Muhammad because they continue his bloodline. The other three caliphs and their descendants carry significance as historical figures for Shiites, but they are not considered to be sources of divine guidance.

According to Shia doctrine, an imam is a perfect example for mankind, appointed by Allah as a spiritual guide. As such, his example *must* be followed in everything.

Wahhabism

There are many schools, orders, sects, and movements within these two branches of Islam. One movement within the Sunni branch of Islam that I believe is worth mentioning here is Wahhabism. Wahhabism is of special concern because of its growing influence in the United States, as well as in the Middle East. This is the dominant form of the religion in Saudi Arabia, Kuwait, and Qatar, and it is even more fundamentalist in its outlook than the Shia faith.

Wahhabism might have faded as an influence on Islam had it not been for the discovery of oil in Saudi Arabia in the 1930s. The vast influx of oil revenues pouring into the Middle East since that time has led to the spread of this most conservative—some would say violent—form of Islam. In fact, wealthy Arabians and even the Saudi government have spent tens of millions of petro-dollars exporting their brand of Islam around the world—including schools and organizations in the United States. They preach a rigid, intolerant version of Islam that breeds radicalism. The pulpits of these mosques are filled with Wahhabi preachers spouting violence against America and all infidels (Christians and Jews).

A Peaceful Religion?

After examining what we know about Muhammad's life, you can see that it can be divided into two parts—the tolerant years in Mecca and the aggressive years in Medina. The Quran reflects those two parts, and that is why at times someone will point out a teaching in the Quran that seems to indicate that Islam teaches adherents to live at peace with their enemies. At first, this was the strategy Muhammad advocated as he preached his revelations from Allah. But as time passed and he saw that attempts to win over Jews through peaceful coexistence were unsuccessful, he came up with a new strategy, one that declared *jihad* (holy war) and conversion to Islam by the sword.

That leads us to question whether those who currently follow the teachings of Muhammad, the founder of Islam, are peaceful or violent. Many Americans have already begun to forget the aftermath of the tragedy of 9/11. On that infamous day in 2001, as we reeled in stunned grief, trying to comprehend the horrors that occurred in New York City, Washington DC, and Pennsylvania, people in other parts of the world were dancing for joy!

Who would do such a thing? The terrorists involved in 9/11 were all radical Islamists who practiced the teachings of the Quran. Islam not only *condones* violence; it *commands* it. A tree is known by its fruit, and the fruit produced by Islam is fourteen hundred years of violence and bloodshed around the world.

What are Muslims taught to do to the people who resist Islam? The Quran says:

> Fight and slay the Pagans wherever you find them, and seize them, beleaguer them, and lie in wait for them in every stratagem (of war).
>
> —Surah 9:5

> The punishment of those who wage war against Allah and His Messenger, and strive with might and main for mischief through the land is: execution, or crucifixion, of the cutting off of hands and feet from opposite sides, or

exile from the land: that is there disgrace in this world, and a heavy punishment is theirs in the Hereafter.

—Surah 5:33

While the majority of the world's 1.5 billion Muslims attempt to live in peace with their neighbors, the number of radicals who preach violence and terror—based on the teaching of the Quran as stated above—is mushrooming around the world. Experts say that 15 to 20 percent of Muslims are radical enough to strap a bomb on their bodies in order to kill Christians and Jews. That means there is an Islamic force of approximately 300 million radicals who are willing to die killing you. We cannot be ignorant of this fact or the recent history that foreshadowed it.

The year 1979 was a watershed for the radicalization of the Middle East, and as we will see in the next chapter, we are reaping the whirlwind of events that unfolded in the following years.

CHAPTER 7

REVOLUTION AND RADICAL ISLAM

Whlle their historic roots go deeper, most of today's well-known Islamic terrorist organizations gained prominence in the late 1970s and early 1980s. One of the key events triggering this increased move toward violence was the 1979 invasion of Afghanistan by the former Soviet Union.

The attempt to subdue the Afghan nation galvanized the beliefs of radicals like Osama bin Laden, a wealthy Saudi Arabian who began to preach that there must be a holy war against the infidels—all those who do not believe in Islam. He supported the Afghan resistance, or *mujahideen*, which would eventually become a full-blown jihad, or holy war. Ironically, the United States also supported the resistance, working with Saudi Arabia and Pakistan to set up Islamic schools in Pakistan for Afghan refugees. These schools later became training centers for Islamic radicals bent on the destruction of the United States and Israel. Americans were unknowingly playing the role of midwife while al Qaeda was in the birth canal.

During that same year, the shah of Iran, who had been put into power with the help of the United States, was forced to flee the country because of growing unrest. His departure paved the way for the late Ayatollah Khomeini, who had been living in exile in Europe, to return to Iran and to bring with him the Islamic revolution. The followers of the ayatollah established an Islamic republic in Iran, seeking to bring about the Islamic Caliphate, formally abolished in 1924, in which there would be one worldwide Islamic community that would apply the religious laws of Islam (*Sharia*) and the tradition of the prophet Muhammad. By so doing, Khomeini set out to wage a war to the death against the contemporary infidels: "the big Satan," the United States, and "the little Satan," Israel.

Late in 1979, the new Iranian regime attacked the U.S. embassy in Iran and took ninety American hostages. Amazingly, President Jimmy Carter, in an act of desperation, reached out to the Palestinian Liberation Organization (PLO), a terrorist organization that had vowed to destroy Israel, to ask for assistance. The Iranians thumbed their noses at a weak and indecisive Carter administration.

The day in January 1981 when Ronald Reagan was sworn into office, Iran released all of the American hostages, believing that Reagan would take the necessary and decisive actions to respond to Iran with military force. The feeble attempts of President Carter to deal with terrorists did much to weaken our country at the time. It was also very damaging to Israel that the Carter administration attempted to work in partnership with a terrorist organization committed to the destruction of Israel.

Since that pivotal year in history, the various branches of the PLO, Osama bin Laden and his al Qaeda organization, the Islamic

Republic of Iran, and a host of other radical Islamic groups have continued to spread terrorism throughout the Middle East and the world. The common thread is their hatred for Jews and, primarily because of America's relationship to Israel, a hatred for the United States. Their commitment to the death of all nonbelievers is well documented. Their actions are clearly based on hatred and evil, and they intend to crush Israel and destroy America.

In 1989 the Soviets finally withdrew from Afghanistan, unable to conquer the rebels. The Taliban, an outgrowth of bin Laden's jihadist efforts, consolidated their control of the country. The Taliban gave sanctuary to bin Laden when Saudi Arabia exiled him over his anti-government activities in relation to U.S. troops, who were temporarily stationed there during the Iraq-Kuwait war. He was deeply angered that "infidels" were allowed to have a presence in the birthplace of Islam. Drawing on organizational efforts he had begun in Afghanistan, bin Laden formed al Qaeda, which has become identified as one of the most dangerous of all of the Islamic terrorist organizations and which claims credit for a number of attacks on the United States and our citizens worldwide, including the 9/11 attack on the World Trade Center in New York and the Pentagon in 2001.

Meanwhile, back in Iran, the revolution continued in full force. The Shiite religious laws and the teachings of its new leader, Khomeini, defined the Jews as infidels and therefore "unclean abominations and Islam's eternal enemies." The continued existence of Israel as a state only added to their desire to strike the United States and Israel. Their hatred of the Jews, who were identified as being allied with the corrupt shah and an ally of the United

States, is and continues to be the central unifying theme of their government. Their false belief that the Palestinians were wronged and illegitimately removed from their own land has been one of the foundations on which the legitimacy of the Islamic regime in Iran is based. Their ultimate goal is the destruction of the State of Israel, proof that there is no real desire for a peace process in the Middle East coming out of Iran or their proxy armies: Hamas in Gaza and Hezbollah in Lebanon.

The dispute with Israel is not about a Palestinian state. The people most responsible for the murders and killings of Americans and Israelites—al Qaeda, Hamas, Hezbollah, and even elements within Fatah—do not want a "Palestinian" State. They are not interested in peace with Israel or even a piece of Israel; they want it all! They want the total destruction of the State of Israel and every Jew face down in the Dead Sea.

Today it is firmly entrenched in the minds of the new Iranian leadership and its president, Mahmoud Ahmadinejad, that the Jews are not just satisfied with having their own nation, but they are essentially scheming to take over the world. Their belief is that, overtly or covertly, the Jews are responsible for every negative situation in the world and that they are behind every international event or crisis, including the Holocaust perpetrated by Nazi Germany.

If this sounds familiar, it is. It is no different than the teachings of the Christian church prior to the Holocaust.

In Iran and among many radical Muslim groups, they often do not even acknowledge the Holocaust as being real. And if it is based in any kind of truth, they argue, it was either a ploy by the Jewish leaders to gain world sympathy or has been greatly exaggerated so that the State of Israel could be formed at the expense of Palestinians.

Jewish control of the media, Hollywood, and most of the news outlets is believed by fundamentalist Islamic groups, both in and outside of Iran, to be a plot by Jews to "control the message." As we read earlier, when the early Roman church needed to find a reason to persecute Jews, they would blame just about anything they felt compelled to use against the Jews.

The viewpoints of these radical terrorists are past the point of being dangerous and now are easily considered delusional and insane. To call them madmen is justified. To attempt to negotiate with them is beyond naïve. It is time to consider a military pre-emptive strike against Iran's nuclear facilities. I repeat, the only way to win a nuclear war is to make sure it never starts.

From December 7, 1941, when we were attacked at Pearl Harbor, until September 11, 2001, when suicide bombers crashed planes into the twin towers in New York, the Pentagon in Virginia, and a field in Pennsylvania, the United States felt relatively free from blatant military actions against us on our own soil. Yes, the bomb shelters of the 1950s were evidence of the growing tensions with the Soviet Union during the cold war, but overall, Americans felt safe at home within our own borders during those sixty years.

For most of that same period of time, Israel was under constant attack either from surrounding nations or the threat of attack from terrorists determined to annihilate them. Suicide car bombs, seemingly random missiles fired on civilian populations, abductions and murder of innocent civilians, mob violence generated by anti-Semitic groups, and images of hatred and anger in the media are too often the way of life in Israel. The shadow of violence over the nation of Israel and the Jewish people worldwide is clearly due to the deep anti-Semitism and hatred of Jews by religious leaders of the radical Islamic groups.

The Anti-Defamation League, an organization formed in 1913 to stop the defamation of Jewish people, maintains a chronology of terrorist attacks on Israel over the past several years. As I looked at the list on their Web site, which includes every kind of terrorist activity imaginable, I felt tears forming in my eyes. I scrolled down the seemingly endless list of atrocities, reading about Israeli children, women, and men who were killed or wounded while going about their daily lives. My heart grew heavy with the reality that hatred is alive and well in the Middle East today and that the same evil that allowed Hitler to rise to power continues to permeate the region.

Some of the most recent stories at the time of this writing include:[1]

- *"January 29, 2007:* Three people were killed in a suicide bombing in a bakery in Eilat, the first suicide bombing in the city. Islamic Jihad claimed responsibility for the attack.

- *"June 25, 2006:* Eliahu Asheri, 18, of Itamar, was kidnapped by Palestinian terrorists from the Popular Resistance Committees while hitchhiking from Betar Illit, southwest of Bethlehem, to Neveh Tzuf, where

he was studying. His body was found on June 29
in Ramallah. Israeli Authorities believe Asheri was
murdered by his captors shortly after his kidnapping.

- *"April 17, 2006:* Nine people were killed and at least
  40 wounded in a suicide bombing near the old central
  bus station in Tel Aviv. The blast ripped through
  Falafel Rosh Ha'ir, the same restaurant that was hit by
  an attack on January 19. The Islamic Jihad and Fatah's
  Al Aksa Martyrs Brigades both claimed responsibility for the attack. The Hamas led PA government
  defended the suicide bombing, calling it an act of 'self-
  defense.' Hamas official spokesman Sami Abu Zuhri
  called the attack 'a natural result of the continued
  Israeli crimes against our people.'

- *"March 30, 2006:* Four people were killed in a suicide
  bombing outside Kedumim in the northern West
  Bank. The Al-Aksa Martyrs Brigades took responsibility for the attack.

- *"January 19, 2006:* At least 30 people were injured in
  a suicide bombing near the old central bus station in
  southern Tel Aviv. Islamic Jihad claimed responsibility
  for the attack.

- *"December 29, 2005:* Three people were killed—two
  Palestinian civilians and an Israeli soldier—in a
  suicide bombing at a checkpoint near Tulkarm. The
  suicide bomber was apparently planning to target one

of the many children's events taking place in Tel Aviv for the Hanukkah holiday, but was stopped at the checkpoint. Islamic Jihad claimed responsibility for the attack."

And the list goes on and on and on.

As the violence escalates, I believe the stage is being set for a battle such as the world has never seen before. The Islamic revolution birthed in Iran in the late seventies is in full force today. The names and faces may have changed—then, the Ayatollah Khomeini; now, Iran's president Mahmoud Ahmadinejad—but the goal remains the same: to wipe Israel, America, and all infidels off the face of the earth.

People often ask me why Israel needs our support. The answer is very simple: their very existence is seriously threatened. With every passing day, the violent threats and rocket attacks on Israel and the Jewish people are growing. The two proxy armies of Iran, Hamas and Hezbollah, are camped on Israel's southern and northern borders, armed to the teeth, waiting for another bloody war. Appeasement is not the answer. You cannot negotiate with leaders and organizations whose written covenants pledge your death and destruction. Not since statehood was declared in 1948 has the security of Israel been at greater risk. They are at war. With every passing day, the threats and violent attacks on Israel and the Jewish people are growing. Appeasement is not the answer. You cannot negotiate with leaders and organizations whose covenants pledge your destruction. Not since statehood was declared in 1948 has the security of Israel been at greater risk.

The Growing Iranian Threat

As I stated in the opening chapter, I believe Iran's President Mahmoud Ahmadinejad is rapidly acquiring the nuclear technology to carry out his threats against Israel, despite intense international opposition. Additionally, Ahmadinejad continues to announce his anti-Semitic stance to the world.

In a UN speech on June 3, 2007, the Iranian president stated that the Lebanese and Palestinians had pressed a "countdown button" to bring an end to the "Zionist regime."

"By God's will," he said, "we will witness the destruction of this regime in the near future." UN Secretary-General Ban Ki-moon expressed shock and dismay at Ahmadinejad's comments and said Israel was "a full and long-standing member of the United Nations with the same rights and obligations as every other member."[2]

If there is any doubt that the president of Iran is committed to the destruction of Israel, we should simply hear his own words. As Hitler made clear his intentions toward the Jews of Europe prior to taking action, I believe President Ahmadinejad of Iran is doing the same in the Middle East today. If we simply choose to ignore the warnings, we will be guilty of the same sin of omission that our predecessors were guilty of as Hitler gathered his forces and made his plans only seventy years ago.

History has taught the Jewish people that when someone threatens to kill you, take him seriously. Haman was followed by Hitler, and now comes Ahmandinejad of Iran. He says what he means and means what he says.

Continued Conflict With Palestinians

The terrorist group Hamas—also committed to destroying Israel—won the Palestinian elections in 2006, taking control of the government and its armed security forces. As I write this book, the situation is so fluid that it is impossible to know who is in charge. The Palestinian lawmakers, after having recently installed a new coalition government to replace Hamas by an overwhelming vote of 83 to 3, are facing continued turmoil within the government. Much of the conflict is based on one faction not being anti-Israeli enough.

The new government—a partnership between Hamas and Fatah, the military wing of the Palestinian Authority—had refused to acknowledge the Jewish state and renounce their violence against it. In fact, the alliance called for a Palestinian state on land the Israelis have occupied since 1967. Israel announced that it would not deal with any coalition that includes Hamas, but will continue to try to identify reasonable people to work with within the alliance.

To keep the situation Israel faces in context, consider that, despite their open hostility to Israel, the Hamas-Fatah alliance had gained some international support. Egypt described the new coalition government as a "precious opportunity to resume the peace process." Syria demanded that the United States, United Nations, European Union, and Russia end their restrictions.[3]

Norway, as an example, had immediately lifted sanctions. Britain and the United Nations suggested they would lend financial support if the coalition can keep violence against Israel in check.

The situation will always be fluid and will be marked by violence and a struggle for dominance between the factions within the Palestinian ranks, making the enforceability of any "peace agreement" unrealistic. This is particularly true with the undue influence Iran is playing in the region, using Hamas in the Palestinian areas and Hezbollah in Lebanon as shadow organizations for its own intentions against Jews.

Israel has called upon the international community "to stand by its own principles and not to deal with a government that refuses to recognize the right of Israel to exist."[4]

Where does America stand? Although the United States has expressed reservations about the Hamas-Fatah coalition government, stating that they must recognize Israel and honor previous agreements with her, U.S. leaders generally support a peace plan that allows for the establishment of a Palestinian state.

By supporting the idea of a Palestinian state, America's leaders are asking the Jewish people to reach out and take the hand of Mahmoud Abbas, head of the Fatah party, a "military wing" of the Palestinian Authority. Abbas follows the footsteps of anti-Semites such as Yasser Arafat, whose legacy is soaked in the blood of innocent Jewish men, women, and children. These people cannot be trusted to be a lasting party to a real peace process. Such trust must be *earned*.

It is earned by recognizing Israel's right to exist, by ceasing and desisting from all acts of terrorism, and by following the rule of law as established by the community of nations. It is time for America to stop asking Israel to give up more land or to make more concessions for peace with terrorist armies and organizations sworn to their destruction.

Asking Israel to work with Fatah and their leader Abbas is

like asking America to give New York to al Qaeda and Osama bin Laden. There is no difference between al Qaeda, Hamas, and Fatah. The terrorists who flew their planes into the twin towers of New York as human sacrifices are no different from the suicide bombers who kill innocent Jewish women and children in Israel when they go to the synagogue and when they go to the market. While Israel will comply with the request, it should be no surprise to any of us when Fatah resumes its violence, just as Arafat did so many times before.

In early 2007 Israeli Defense Forces (IDF) statistical reports indicated there had been a total of 22,406 terrorist attacks on Israel, the West Bank, and the Gaza Strip since September 2000. This is what life in Israel is like on a daily basis.

Americans need to remember that ever since Israel has been a state, legitimately recognized by the international community, they have been at constant war in an effort to defend themselves. They have lived with one terrorist attack after another. It's time, as friends, for us to say, "Israel, we stand with you—and enough is enough! You have the right to attack your terrorist enemies just as America has the right to attack ours!"

The Iraq Study Group Report

With mounting pressures on the Bush administration to bring peace to the Middle East at any cost, more and more Americans are calling for the United States to pull our troops out of Iraq. This growing frustration among Americans over the war in Iraq is what cost the Republicans control of Congress in 2006. When Bush announced that he was sending an additional 30,000 troops to Iraq as part of a surge strategy to quell the violence in Baghdad, the frustration of many Americans turned to anger.

In one recent anti-war protest in Washington, protesters held signs that read, "Jail to the chief!" and "Impeach Bush for war crimes!" while they chanted, "Troops out now!"[5]

With the publication of *The Iraq Study Group Report* by James Baker and Lee Hamilton in 2006, this pressure to end the war in Iraq is joined hand in hand with the pressure to allow a two-state solution in Israel and the West Bank. The West Bank is the highly disputed strip of land along the west bank of the Jordan River, which includes the Old City of Jerusalem, the Western Wall, and Hebron, the burial ground of the biblical patriarchs. The biblical names for this territory are Judea and Samaria.

Baker's perspective is that we must first find a peaceful resolution in the West Bank before we can bring about a peaceful solution in Iraq. Baker has never been pro-Israel on any issue throughout his political career.

This view implies that the Arab-Israeli conflict is the root of all of the instability in the entire Mideast region—an assertion that could not be further from the truth. What does Israel have to do with al Qaeda attacks on Shia Muslims in Iraq? What does Sudan's policy of genocide in Darfur have to do with Israel? This warped thinking is exactly what the enemies of Israel use to divert the attention of Americans away from the real sources of instability in the Middle East—like the Islamic revolution that continues unabated in Iran.

The Iraq Study Group Report suggests that Israel give up the

Golan Heights. This recommendation is no doubt intended to gain the cooperation of Syria in matters relating to Iraq. Even if it were acceptable that Israel give up this land—which it most definitely is *not*—the study group never calls for the dismantling of anti-Israel terrorist organizations in Syria; it simply asks for them to stop supplying arms to groups such as Hamas and Hezbollah while allowing them to remain open for business—the business of "wiping Israel off the map."

The Iraq Study Group Report is an ill-conceived document, and its recommendations for Israel clearly violate the Word of God. How so? Joel 3:2 says, "I will also gather all nations [this includes America], and bring them down to the Valley of Jehoshaphat; and I will enter into judgment with them there on account of My people, My heritage Israel...they have also divided up My land."

If America forces Israel to give up the Golan Heights or the West Bank (Judea and Samaria), it will clearly violate Scripture. We are giving the enemies of Israel the high ground in the coming war for Israel's survival. It's time for our national leaders in Washington to stop this madness.

Israel should not give up another inch of land until every anti-Israel terrorist organization lays down its weapons of war and proves that it is willing to live in peace side by side with the nation of Israel.

Every Christian in America has a biblical mandate to stand in absolute solidarity with Israel and demand that our leaders in Washington stop recommending Israel's withdrawal as the solution to every conflict that arises in the Middle East. Regardless of what is to be done to bring closure to America's military involvement in Iraq, our government must never adopt policies that will leave Israel weaker and her enemies emboldened.

Voices are calling for the sacred city of Jerusalem to be shared as part of a "road map for peace" in the Middle East. Let it be known to all men far and near that the city of Jerusalem is not up for negotiation with anyone at any time for any reason in the future. It has been and shall always be the eternal and undivided capital of the State of Israel.

After the return of Israel from Babylonian captivity, when people from other nations sought to share in the restoration of Jerusalem, Nehemiah, the Jewish governor, said to them: "The God of heaven Himself will prosper us; therefore we His servants will arise and build, but *you have no heritage or right or memorial in Jerusalem*" (Nehemiah 2:20, emphasis added). It is important to see this notation—the nations of the world have no inheritance in Jerusalem.

As the pressure for Middle East peace at any cost continues to build, those who support Israel may quickly become the minority in America. This makes it all the more urgent for Christians in America to understand why we must support Israel and the Jewish people.

Let me close this section with a brief overview of some of the major groups pledged to the destruction of Israel and the United States.

Islamic Terrorist Groups

Today, jihad is the world's foremost source of terrorism, inspiring a worldwide campaign of violence by self-proclaimed jihadist groups.

There are many more terrorist groups than I have room to talk about in the remainder of this chapter, but the following is a brief listing of the key militant groups in the Mideast region.

Al Qaeda

The international influence of Osama bin Laden and his al Qaeda network spans the globe. Al Qaeda (Arabic for "the foundation" or "the base") is an Islamic terror organization that began operations in 1988, primarily out of Afghanistan and Pakistan.

Though the number of people involved and the actual structure of al Qaeda are both unknown, American authorities have formulated a rough picture of how the group is said to be organized: Bin Laden is the senior operations chief, and he is advised by a council of about thirty senior al Qaeda members. There is a military committee that trains operatives, acquires weapons, and plans attacks; a financial committee that handles spending (in *The 9/11 Commission Report*, it was estimated that al Qaeda requires $30 million per year to operate); a legal committee that reviews Islamic law; and a committee that issues *fatwa* (religious edicts).[6]

Hezbollah

Hezbollah ("Party of God") is a Shia Muslim political party and paramilitary organization that emerged in the early 1980s. Based in Lebanon, the organization has become the leading radical Islamic movement. Hezbollah's main goal is driving Israeli troops from Lebanon and liberating what it calls its "occupied territory."

Hezbollah is synonymous with terror, suicide bombings, and kidnappings, and it has publicly announced that it is ready to launch a second attack against Israel in support of the Palestinian *intifada* (Arabic for "uprising"). The party is condoned by neighboring Syria and is backed by Iran, which provides it with arms and money.

Armed Islamic Group

The Armed Islamic Group is a terrorist organization seeking to replace the Algerian government with an Islamic state. The group began operations in 1992 after the military government ignored election results that gave victory to the Islamic Salvation Front, the largest Islamic opposition party, in December 1991.

Al-Gama'a al-Islamiyya

Another group to keep tabs on is a militant Egyptian Islamist movement that is considered a terrorist organization by the United States, European Union, and the Egyptian governments. Al-Gama'a al-Islamiyya is dedicated to establishing an Islamic state in Egypt. They began operations in the late 1970s and usually target government buildings, police, the military, tourists, and minorities.

Islamic Jihad

The Islamic Jihad is one of the most complex and dangerous of the Arab terrorist organizations. It is an uncoordinated network of individual groups who generally act on their own initiative, united by a common fundamentalist Islamic ideology that declares holy war (jihad) against the infidels.

At times, the Islamic Jihad groups collaborate closely with the Iranian regime as well as various Palestinian organizations, receiving both guidance and financial aid.[7]

Their ultimate goal is to overthrow all secular Arab governments in order to establish an Islamic pan-Arab empire. Islamic Jihad views the annihilation of the Jews and Israel as an essential step toward fulfilling the goals of Islam.

Hamas

Hamas ("Islamic Resistance Movement") is an Arabic acronym that means "zeal." Hamas is an Islamic party of the Palestinian Authority. Created in 1987, Hamas is known for its suicide bombings and other attacks directed against Israeli civilians, as well as military and security forces targets. The charter of Hamas (written in 1988 and still in effect) calls for the destruction of the State of Israel and the establishment of a Palestinian Islamic state in the area that is now Israel, the West Bank, and the Gaza Strip. The charter states: "There is no solution for the Palestinian question except through Jihad."[8]

According to the U.S. State Department, the group is funded by Iran, Palestinian expatriates, and private benefactors in Saudi Arabia and other Arab states.

Harkat ul-Mujahideen

Harkat-ul-Mujahideen is a Pakistani Islamist terror group. It was established in 1985 in opposition to the Soviet presence in Afghanistan. It claims to be a jihadist organization with the objective of providing awareness with regard to jihad. In addition to being anti-Semitic and anti-Christian, it is an anti-Hindu organization.

Jaish-i-Muhammad

Jaish-i-Muhammad ("Army of Muhammad") is a terrorist organization founded in 2000 that seeks to secure release of imprisoned fellow militants using kidnappings and other terrorist activities to achieve its goals.

All of these groups pose a threat not just to Israel, but to America as well, because of our long-standing support for the Jewish state. To further underscore the compelling reasons to stand in defense of Israel, let us turn now to the debt that society as a whole, and Christianity in particular, owes to the Jewish people.

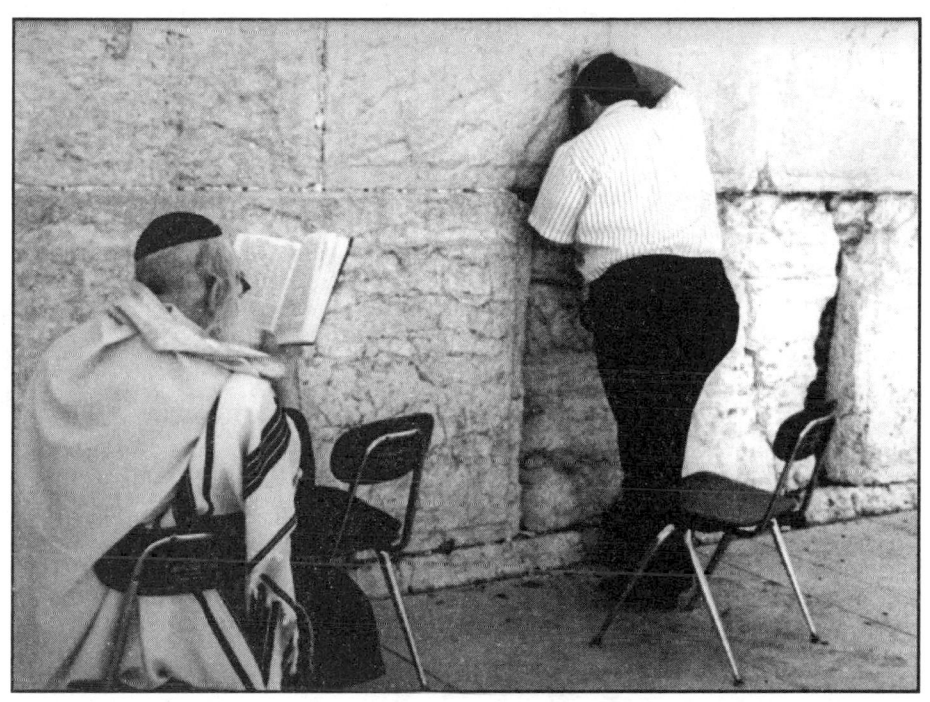

Pastor John Hagee praying at the Western Wall during his first
trip to Israel in 1978. Pictured at left is the unknown worshiper
who inspired Hagee to do something to bring Christians
and Jews together in defense of Israel.

Rabbi Aryeh Scheinberg teaches Pastor John Hagee how to blow the shofar just prior to the first Night to Honor Israel in 1981.

John Hagee; Prime Minister Menachem Begin and
his wife, Aliza; and Diana Hagee in 1981.

Prime Minister Yitzhak Shamir and John Hagee in 1983.

John Hagee with General Ariel Sharon, hero of the
1967 Six-Day War, in the general's office in 1983.

John Hagee and Yitzhak Rabin in 1985.
Prime Minister Rabin was assassinated in 1995.

Benjamin Netanyahu, John Hagee, A Night to Honor Israel 2004.

John and Diana Hagee with Daniel Ayalon, Israeli
Ambassador to the USA, and his wife, Anne, in 2005.

CHAPTER 8

OUR DEBT TO THE JEWISH PEOPLE

C HRISTIANITY COULD NOT AND WOULD NOT EXIST IF IT WERE not for the Jewish people. That concept flies in the face of the anti-Semitic poison that has filled the mouths of church leaders for centuries. But it's true: the Christian values we now hold dear are rooted in the theology practiced by the Israelites for thousands of years before Christianity was in the picture. Their contributions are the bedrock of our very faith.

Jesus Was Jewish

It is essential for anti-Semites to separate Jesus from his Jewish roots, for if you do that, then hatred becomes fashionable and anti-Semitism becomes a Christian virtue. As I said earlier, an anti-Semitic Christian is an oxymoron. An anti-Semite in that context is a dead Christian whose hatred has strangled his faith. Like a chameleon, anti-Semitism can masquerade alternately as "doing the will of God" or political ideology.

If Jesus can be separated from his Jewish roots, then Christians can continue to praise the dead Jews of the past (Abraham, Isaac, and Jacob) while snubbing the Goldbergs across the street. But when you correctly see the Jewish people as the family of our Lord, they become our extended family whom we are commanded to love unconditionally.

Adolf Hitler recognized that he needed to destroy the Jewish roots of Jesus in the minds of the German people. Out of his demented mind came the Mischlinge Regulation, which legally defined a Jew as someone with two Jewish parents. Hitler did this for two reasons. One, he had to absolve Jesus of being Jewish by recognizing Jesus was born exclusively of the Virgin Mary. Nazi goons would never have enthusiastically murdered six million of our Lord's relatives. Second, Hitler feared he was partly Jewish.

John Toland, Pulitzer Prize–winning historian, records in his two-volume history *Adolf Hitler* that Hitler's father's birth certificate declared him to be "illegitimate." The space for the father's name on the birth certificate was left blank, generating a mystery that remains unsolved.

Indeed, there is a distant possibility that Hitler's grandfather was a wealthy Jew named Frankenberger or Frankenreither. Hitler was so concerned about the matter that he ordered his personal attorney, Hans Frank, to investigate the matter confidentially. The subsequent report, gathered from "all possible sources," greatly disturbed Hitler. Frank's report to the Führer concluded, regretfully, the possibility could not be dismissed that Hitler's father was half-Jewish. If true, then Hitler would have been a non-Aryan crossbreed, or *mischling*. And if true, then Hitler would fit the historical pattern of half-Jews who have tormented the Jewish people from the beginning of time.

The Mischlinge Regulation removed the stigma of Hitler's Jewish past, since it meant he did not meet the requirements for being a Jew according to his new definition. The Regulation also separated Jesus from the Jews of Germany. (Because of Mary's immaculate conception, Jesus had just one Jewish parent.) Hitler made hating Jews "the will of God." He wrote in *Mein Kampf*, "Hence today I believe that I am acting in accordance with the will of the Almighty Creator: by defending myself against the Jew, I am fighting for the *work of the Lord*."[1]

Most Christians think of Jesus and his disciples as Christians before their time. Not so! Jesus was not a Christian. He was born to Jewish parents, he was dedicated in the Jewish tradition, he was reared studying the words of Moses and the prophets of Israel, he became a Jewish rabbi, and he died with a sign over his head written in three languages: "This is the king of the Jews!"

Jesus died without ever hearing the word *Christian*. The Bible first records its use in Antioch, forty years after the crucifixion (Acts 11:26), to describe Jesus's followers. The word was used by the heathen to describe the loving conduct of those who followed the teachings of this gentle Jewish rabbi. I can only imagine what word would be coined by nonbelievers today to describe Christian conduct one toward the other.

If Jesus Christ came to your church this Sunday morning, would the ushers let him enter the front door? Perhaps not. He would appear small and slender with penetrating dark eyes, an olive complexion, and prominent Semitic features. He would have the long falling earlocks of the Hebrews, his hair uncut at the corners, and a full manly beard, and his shoulders would be draped with a *tallit* (prayer shawl), whose message yet remains a mystery to most of Christianity.

If Jesus identified himself to your congregation as a Jewish rabbi who befriended prostitutes, who socialized with tax collectors and other outcasts, who was hated by the government, and who surrounded himself with twelve full-bearded, unemployed men with shoulder-length hair, could they get a seat? Probably not!

If he commanded your wealthiest church members to sell all they had to give to the poor, or if he entered your beautiful church gym and turned over the bingo tables, shouting, "My house is a house of prayer" (Luke 19:46), would your ushers call the police? I have no doubt they would.

The simple truth is, after two thousand years of anti-Semitic teaching and preaching, we have lost sight of the Jewish nature of our Lord and Savior, Jesus Christ.

Just how Jewish was Jesus?

His Parents Were Jewish

Jesus of Nazareth was of the tribe of Judah, which is linked to King David, Abraham, and Moses (Matthew 1:1–2). His name was given to Mary by an angel of God. *Jesus* (*Yeshua* in Hebrew) means "the Lord saves." *Christ* is the term that identifies him as the "Anointed One."

Mary and Joseph raised Jesus according to the cultural and spiritual traditions of Jewish society. He was taken to the temple to be circumcised on the eighth day, which was (and still is) a very Jewish event (Luke 2:21). At the end of his twelfth year, which would have been his thirteenth birthday, Jesus was taken to the temple for his bar mitzvah, which was (and still is) the custom of the Jews (Luke 2:42). Jesus went into the temple a boy, but he came out of the temple a man.

In that context, it is not hard to understand the controversial conversation between Jesus and his mother following the occasion. When Mary and Joseph left the temple and discovered after one day's journey that Jesus was not with them, they returned to the temple to find their son in a dialogue with scholars. Mary scolded Jesus, saying, "Son, why have You done this to us? Your father and I have sought You anxiously." Jesus answered, "Why did you seek Me?" (Luke 2:48–49).

Some Christians see Jesus's response as being disrespectful to his mother. But he was not being disrespectful. Jesus was now a man, and his mother was having difficulty adjusting to the fact. Some things never change!

Many Christian teachers say that because the Bible is silent about the life of Jesus from this event to the beginning of his public ministry, we know nothing about the life of Jesus from his twelfth year until he was thirty. This absence of a biblical record has even led to some bizarre, esoteric teachings that Jesus traveled to Egypt and studied Eastern-style religions during those years.

But that is simply not the case. Because Jesus was Jewish, we know exactly what he was doing at every phase of his life. From *Everyman's Talmud* we read:

> At five years the age is reached for the study of scripture; at ten for the study of Mishnah; at thirteen for the fulfillment of the Commandments [bar mitzvah]; at fifteen for the study of Talmud; at eighteen for marriage; at twenty for seeking a livelihood; at thirty for entering into one's full strength [life's work].[2]

Jesus, therefore, began studying the scriptures at the age of five; he studied the *Mishnah*, the written record of oral Jewish traditions, at the age of ten and was bar mitzvahed at age thirteen in the temple. At fifteen, he studied the Talmud, the rabbinic commentaries on the law. Knowing the cross was before him, Jesus did not marry at the customary age of eighteen. At twenty, he worked as a carpenter with his father Joseph, and he began public ministry at age thirty, having reached his full strength, or what is considered the age of maturity.

Jesus Practiced Traditional Judaism

Those who say that Jesus did not practice traditional Judaism have no knowledge of history or Scripture. The fact is, Judaism was the only faith on the face of the earth during the life of Jesus that believed in a single omnipotent Supreme Being. The only theology God ever created was Judaism! It was the lone voice of Judaism that shouted to a pagan world saturated with polytheistic deities, "Hear, O Israel, the Lord our God is One."

It was Judaism that believed man was created in God's image. It was traditional Judaism that gave us the concepts of hell, heaven, angels, devils, the acceptance of Adam and Eve as the first man and woman, the creation of the world in seven days, and even its age, four thousand years.

It was Judaism that taught us to sing while other religions wail in sorrow. It was Judaism that gave us love and respect for life. While pagan religions sacrificed their children to foreign gods, Judaism gave us a loving God who adored the life of every child.

It was Judaism that gave us the Lord's Supper, which is a part of the Passover celebration, commemorating the breaking of bread and taking the Communion cup. Early Christians celebrated the Passover for three hundred years after the death of Jesus—until Constantine made it illegal in an effort to separate Jews from Gentiles.

It was Judaism that gave us the patriarchs, the prophets, the Scripture, and our Lord. For that reason, Rabbi Jesus of Nazareth said, "Salvation is of the Jews" (John 4:22). Every word of the New Testament verifies that Jesus, his family, and his disciples practiced traditional Judaism in their daily lives.

Jewish People Gave Us the Scriptures

Every word of the *Tanakh*, the Jewish Bible (which is the Christian Old Testament), was written by Jewish people. It is the light of truth and reason upon which our society and civilization is built.

George Washington said, "It is impossible to rightly govern the world without God and the Bible."[3]

Abraham Lincoln said, "I believe the Bible is the best gift God has given to man. All the good Savior gave to the world was communicated through this Book."[4]

Daniel Webster said, "If there is anything in my thoughts or style to commend, the credit is due to my parents for instilling in me an early love of the Scriptures. If we abide by the principles taught in the Bible, our country will go on prospering and to prosper; but if we and our posterity neglect its instructions and authority, no man can tell how sudden a catastrophe may overwhelm us and bury all our glory in profound obscurity."[5]

Before the current obsession with UFOs, the pens of Isaiah and Jeremiah recorded the story of Elijah being transported from Earth in a space vehicle in the original "Chariot of Fire" (2 Kings 2:11).[6]

Before the movie *Jaws* emptied the beaches of the world with its celluloid terrorism, the pen of Jonah recorded how he was swallowed alive by a "great fish" and spent three days and nights in its stomach before being vomited out on dry land.

The Bible is a book of poetry, history, love, sex, romance, war, adventure, and an introduction to the living God of heaven. To sum it all up, the Jewish people gave to Christianity the foundation of the Word of God. The Jewish people gave to us the patriarchs— Abraham, Isaac, and Jacob. The Jewish people gave to us the disciples. The Jewish people gave to us the apostle Paul, who wrote most of the New Testament.

Without the Jewish contribution to Christianity, there would be no Christianity. Think about this: the Jewish people do not need Christianity to explain their existence, but we cannot explain our existence without our Jewish roots.

Society's debt to Judaism goes beyond the Christian faith. The entire world, and especially the United States, owes a debt to the Jewish people. The contributions of the Jewish people are staggering, especially considering their minuscule number.

Popular American writer Mark Twain said of the Jewish people:

> ...If statistics are right, the Jews constitute but one percent of the human race. It suggests a nebulous dim puff of stardust lost in the blaze of the Milky Way. Properly, the Jew ought hardly to be heard of; but he is heard of, has always been heard of. He is as prominent on the planet as any other people, and his commercial importance is extravagantly out of proportion to the smallness of his bulk. His contributions to the world's list of great names in literature, science, art, music, finance, medicine and abstruse learning are also away out of proportion to the weakness of his numbers. He has made a marvelous fight in this world, in all the ages; and has done it with his hands tied behind him. He could be vain of himself and be excused for it.
>
> The Egyptian, the Babylonian, and the Persian rose, filled the planet with sound and splendor, then faded to dream-stuff and passed away; the Greek and the Roman followed; and made a vast noise, and they are gone; other people have sprung up and held their torch high for a time, but it burned out, and they sit in twilight now, or have vanished. The Jew saw them all, beat them all, and is now what he always was, exhibiting no decadence, no infirmities of age, no weakening of his parts, no slowing of his

energies, no dulling of his alert and aggressive mind. All things are mortal but the Jew; all other forces pass, but he remains. What is the secret of his immortality?[7]

The answer to Twain's question about the secret of the Jews' immortality lies in the supernatural power of God. Jehovah God created the Jewish nation and attached to them this promise: "In you all the families of the earth shall be blessed" (Genesis 12:3).

The Bible and world history testify that the Jewish people have blessed the nations of the earth. Here are a few highlights of the Jewish contributions to society at large and to America.

The Jewish Contribution to Society

As of statistics gathered and published in 2006, the world's population is estimated at 6.5 billion people. Jewish people worldwide represent only .23 percent of the human race compared to Christians, who make up 33 percent, and Muslims, who make up 20 percent.[8] As Mark Twain surmised over a century ago, based on the population of the Jews in proportion to the rest of the world, it's surprising that we hear about them at all beyond a brief mention in a high-school geography class.

Yet throughout history, Jews have been at the center of most of the world's creative, scientific, and cultural achievements. They are disproportionately high as Nobel Prize recipients, they are overrepresented in the field of medicine, and their contributions in the area of scientific research and discovery are staggering.

Consider this small snapshot of Jewish accomplishments:

- Leonardo da Vinci: all-around genius, inventor, artist, and scientist; evidence of Jewish mother
- Camille Pissarro: father of impressionism
- Shel Silverstein: author of children's stories; poet
- Anne Frank: author/diarist
- Arthur Miller: playwright
- Elie Wiesel: author; Nobel Prize for Peace recipient
- Ayn Rand: author
- J. D. Salinger: author, *The Catcher in the Rye*
- Isaac Bashevis Singer: Nobel Prize for Literature recipient
- William James Sidis: smartest person on earth, with IQ of 250–300
- Milton Hershey: founder of Hershey's Chocolate
- Michael Dell: philanthropist, founder of Dell Computer
- Steve Ballmer: CEO of Microsoft
- Paul Warburg: founder of Federal Reserve Banking System
- Leonard Bernstein: composer, conductor
- Felix Mendelssohn: composer, musical genius
- Arthur Fiedler: renowned conductor of Boston Pops
- John Kemeny: mathematician; coinventor of the BASIC computer programming language
- Emile Berliner: inventor of the gramophone (record player) and the telephone microphone

- Jonas Salk: inventor of the first polio vaccine
- Albert Sabin: developer of an improved live polio vaccine
- Sigmund Freud: father of psychoanalysis

Actually, this is only a small representation of the accomplishments of the Jewish people in society at large. The honest fact is, if an anti-Semite had the courage to truly boycott everything Jewish, his life would regress to the Dark Ages. Our technology, music, movies, books, and clothes are all created with significant Jewish involvement, and the health—and even the very lives—of many rely on discoveries by Jewish medical scientists. With all of the life-saving and life-enhancing objects contributed by Jews that have become a part of our everyday lives, anti-Semites are doomed as hypocrites.

While most of the contributions listed above are appreciated by our modern culture, one of the largest contributions from the Jewish people was made four thousand years ago, and it affected the future of all of the world's civilizations. This contribution is the concept of monotheism, discussed in chapter 6.

Before Abraham, Isaac, Jacob, and their descendants formed the nation of Israel, the rest of the world's civilizations were trapped in polytheism, the belief in multiple gods. Christians and even Muslims, building upon the Jewish concept of one God, have spread worldwide the concepts of monotheism and one absolute standard of right and wrong—a standard that originated with the Jews.

What we today call Judeo-Christian values had their roots in God's words to the Jewish patriarchs as recorded in Scripture. These

Judeo-Christian values have provided the foundation of liberal democracy during the last 230 years. America's Founding Fathers used the Bible as a source of inspiration and a basis for values, as evidenced in these words from the Declaration of Independence:

> We hold these truths to be self-evident, that all men are created equal, that they are endowed by their Creator with certain unalienable Rights, that among these are Life, Liberty, and the pursuit of Happiness.[9]

The democratic government and human rights that form the American way of life and the foundation of all Western thinking are based on the concept of one God. What a profound contribution to the world!

The Jewish Contribution to America

In 1492, King Ferdinand and Queen Isabella of Spain signed the Edict of Expulsion, demanding that the Jews of Spain convert to Christianity or be expelled from Spain. The Jewish people were forced again to look for a new home. That search began as Jewish businessmen funded a sailor named Christopher Columbus.

A great deal of speculation swirls around the possibility that Columbus may have been Jewish, or at least of Jewish descent. The *Encyclopedia Britannica* references that he may have come from a Spanish-Jewish family that settled in Genoa, Italy. What some consider to be compelling evidence of his Jewish ties is the fact that he began the account of his voyage to the New World with a reference to the expulsion of the Jews from Spain:

> In the same month in which their Majesties issued the edict that all Jews should be driven out of the kingdom and its territories, in the same month they gave me the order to undertake with sufficient men my expedition of discovery to the Indies.[10]

In one document Columbus refers to the second temple in Jerusalem by the Hebraic term "Second House," and he dates this destruction as the year 68 in accordance with Jewish tradition. Columbus also seems to have deliberately delayed the day of his sailing until August 3 so he would not be sailing on the Ninth of Av, which is the anniversary of the destruction of the temple.

Whether Columbus himself was Jewish or not, what is certain is that he had Jewish friends. Some scholars believe that Columbus's Spanish-Jewish friends, such as Luis de Santangel and Don Isaac Abravanel, were responsible for garnering Columbus an audience with Queen Isabella, convincing the Spanish monarchs to approve his proposals and provide financing for his trip to the New World. Several passengers on the famous voyage to the New World were Jewish as well.

As Spain closed its doors to the Jews, a door into a New World was opening to what would in time become America. The hands that pulled the door open were Jewish.

Funding for the American Revolution

During the American Revolution, when George Washington and the Continental Army were fighting for their very lives in the snows of Valley Forge, they didn't have enough food to eat, they didn't have enough weapons, and they didn't have enough ammunition to fight the British. It looked as if the declaration of life, liberty, and the pursuit of happiness would never bear fruit. Haym Salomon, a Jewish patriot and banker, went to the Jewish people of America and Europe and raised millions of dollars. He gave the money he raised to George Washington, and that contribution turned the tide of the American Revolution.[11]

According to some, Haym Salomon may have been the true author of the first draft of the U.S. Constitution. Some also speculate that Salomon was the designer of the Great Seal of United States of America, as shown on the dollar bill.

It is unclear whether these claims about Salomon are based in legend or in truth. Whatever Salomon's full contribution to American history, I believe an acknowledgment of our forefathers' gratitude to Salomon and other Jewish patriots is revealed upon close examination of the seal. Above the head of the American eagle, the thirteen stars representing America's thirteen colonies form the shape of the Star of David.

Preservation of Jefferson's Monticello

Uriah P. Levy was a Jewish patriot and U.S. naval officer during the War of 1812. Levy regarded Thomas Jefferson as one of the greatest men in history. In 1826, Levy purchased Jefferson's estate, Monticello, which had become so run-down during the ten years since Jefferson's death that it was virtually in ruin. Levy began restoring the buildings and grounds, including the purchase of an additional 2,500 acres adjoining the historic property. After Levy's death in 1862, his will directed that Monticello and the adjoining property be left to the people of the United States. What we now enjoy as a landmark of American history is the result of a Jewish man's willingness to spare no expense in order to preserve a national treasure for the people of America.

Timeless tribute to Lady Liberty

In 1883 great American writers such as Walt Whitman and Mark Twain contributed original manuscripts to an exhibition raising money for the Statue of Liberty's pedestal. A budding young poet contributed a sonnet called "The New Colossus," written just a few days earlier. The immortal words were penned by Emma Lazarus, a Jewish American, soon after her return from a European trip where she had seen the persecution of Jews and others firsthand. Her passionate words that would forever identify Lady Liberty as the "Mother of Exiles" were immortalized in a plaque that was added to the base of the statue in 1903:

> Not like the brazen giant of Greek fame,
> With conquering limbs astride from land to land;
> Here at our sea-washed, sunset gates shall stand
> A mighty woman with a torch, whose flame
> Is the imprisoned lightning, and her name
> Mother of Exiles. From her beacon-hand
> Glows world-wide welcome; her mild eyes command
> The air-bridged harbor that twin cities frame.
>
> "Keep ancient lands, your storied pomp!" cries she
> With silent lips. "Give me your tired, your poor,
> Your huddled masses yearning to breathe free,
> The wretched refuse of your teeming shore,
> Send these, the homeless, tempest-tost to me.

I lift my lamp beside the golden door!"[12]

—Emma Lazarus, 1883

World War II and the atomic bomb

Albert Einstein, Jewish physicist, author of the theory of relativity, and Nobel Prize winner, was born in the German town of Ulm. In January 1933, Hitler came to power, and Einstein promptly resigned from his position at the Royal Academy of Sciences and never returned to Germany. A deeply religious man, Einstein was convinced that "the less knowledge a scholar possesses, the further he feels from God. But the greater his knowledge, the nearer his approach to God."[13]

During World War II, secret news reached the physicist, now residing in the United States, that the German uranium project was progressing and the prospects of the Nazis having a super-weapon produced by atomic energy was very possible.

Einstein signed a letter that pointed out the feasibility of atomic energy. It was this letter addressed to President Franklin Roosevelt that sparked the Manhattan Project and gave birth to atomic energy. The genius that birthed the formula $E=mc^2$ and later put an end to the atrocities of World War II was Jewish. Military experts estimate that approximately seven hundred fifty thousand lives of American soldiers were saved that would have been lost in a full-scale military invasion of Japan.

America's unofficial national anthem

Legendary songwriter Irving Berlin was born to Jewish parents in Russia in 1888. An anti-Semitic pogrom forced his parents and their eight children, including Irving, to emigrate from Russia to the United States in 1894. As the son of Russian immigrants in New York City, Berlin only received two years of formal education and never learned to read music, yet he became one of the greatest songwriters of our time. Berlin composed the words and music of more than 1,500 songs—including the beloved classic "White Christmas" and America's unofficial national anthem, "God Bless America."

In 1944, the National Conference of Christians and Jews honored Berlin for his efforts to "eliminate religious and racial conflict." Ten years later, President Dwight Eisenhower presented Berlin with the Congressional gold medal in recognition of the song "God Bless America."

Other Jewish contributions

The Jewish contribution continued in America through the lives of Supreme Court Justices Felix Frankfurter and Louis Brandeis. Medical journals bulge with the names of Jewish physicians whose medical discoveries have saved tens of thousands of lives. In spite of their small number, they have dominated many of the major fields of human endeavor: merchants, humanitarians, scientists, astronauts, statesmen, educators, writers, musicians, and gifted entertainers who have blessed our lives with their God-given genius.

These people are a living testimony of God's promise to Abraham: "In thee shall all the nations of the earth be blessed" (Genesis 12:3, KJV).

Some Quick Facts About Israel's Leadership in Medical Research
Israelis developed a shunt that is now providing relief for people who suffer from glaucoma.
Israeli researchers have found that combining electrical stimulation and chemotherapy makes cancerous metastases disappear.
Israeli researchers have developed the first vaccine against West Nile virus.
Israeli scientists have developed a DNA nano-computer that detects cancer and releases drugs to treat the disease.
Israeli researchers are developing a five-year flu vaccine in the form of a nose drop.[14]

Some Quick Facts About Israel's Leadership in Technological Research and Development
The cell phone was developed in Israel.
Most of the Windows NT operating system was developed in Israel.
The Pentium MMX chip technology was designed in Israel.
Voice mail technology was developed in Israel.
The technology for AOL Instant Messenger was developed in 1996 by four young Israelis.
The first PC anti-virus software was developed in Israel in 1979.[15]

Some Quick Facts About Israel's Leadership in Technological Research and Development
Israel produces more scientific papers per capita than any other nation—109 per 10,000—as well as one of the highest per capita rates of patents filed.[16]
Israel has the third highest rate of entrepreneurship—and the highest rate among women and among people over the age of fifty-five—in the world.[17]

Our indebtedness to the Jewish people is but one reason we must support the State of Israel. But the most important reason of all is the fact that honoring Israel brings the blessing of God.

CHAPTER 9

HONORING ISRAEL BRINGS GOD'S BLESSING

I N THE PREVIOUS CHAPTER, I MENTIONED SOME OF THE WAYS the Jewish people have blessed our society by their many scientific, medical, and social contributions. Now I want to show you in Scripture some details of how this blessing is transmitted.

The Bible states quite clearly, "I will bless those who bless you, and I will curse him who curses you" (Genesis 12:3). Entire books could be written on how that blessing and cursing have dramatically impacted human history. It is an undeniable fact that the man or the nation that has blessed Israel has been blessed of God, and to the man or the nation that cursed Israel the judgment of God came in spades.

Several combined scriptures verify that prosperity (Genesis 12:3; Psalm 122:6), divine healing (Luke 7:1–5), and salvation and the outpouring of the Holy Spirit (Acts 10) came first to Gentiles who blessed the Jewish people and the nation of Israel in a practical manner. Paul expands on this teaching in Romans 15:27. Let's take a look at some other biblical examples.

God Blesses the Gentiles Through the Jews

A Gentile named Laban was the Syrian father-in-law of the patriarch Jacob. Laban abused Jacob by changing his wages ten times, each time to Jacob's hurt. He also tricked Jacob into working fourteen years for the hand of his daughter Rachel. Laban, in the biblical text, is a deceitful, fraudulent, and untrustworthy employer.

After more than fourteen years of this abuse, Jacob, the employee, comes to Laban, the employer, and submits his resignation. The words Laban spoke when he realized he was about to lose Jacob as an employee reveal a divine truth that yet remains upon the earth. That truth is that God blesses the Gentiles through the Jewish people.

> And Laban said unto him [Jacob], "Please stay, if I have found favor in your eyes, for I have learned by experience that the Lord has *blessed me for your sake*."
>
> —Genesis 30:27, emphasis added

Egypt Blessed Because of Joseph

The next prominent person who learned the principle that God blesses the Gentiles through the Jewish people was the exalted ruler of ancient Egypt. Joseph was a Jewish ambassador, sent by God into a distant country to bless the Gentiles and to preserve the nations of the world.

One Jewish boy went down into Egypt in chains by camel caravan, having been sold by his ten jealous older brothers to Midianite merchants passing through Canaan. The teenager was sold for twenty shekels of silver. When the merchants arrived in Egypt, Joseph was sold a second time on the open slave market. His new owner was an Egyptian official named Potiphar, the captain of Pharaoh's guard.

The favor of God was with Joseph, and he rose to a position of responsibility as the business manager of Potiphar's vast estate. It is recorded in Scripture that:

> The LORD blessed the Egyptian's house *for Joseph's sake;*
> and the blessing of the LORD was on all that he had in the
> house and in the field.
>
> —Genesis 39:5, emphasis added

Eventually, after Joseph had been betrayed, imprisoned, and then miraculously released, Pharaoh appointed Joseph as the prime minister of Egypt with these words:

> So Pharaoh asked them [his officials], "Can we find anyone like this man, one in whom is the spirit of God?" Then Pharaoh said to Joseph, "Since God has made all this known unto you, there is no one so discerning and wise as you. You shall be in charge of my palace, and all my people are to submit to your orders. Only with respect to the throne will I be greater than you."
>
> —Genesis 41:38–40, NIV

Pharaoh put the massive gold signet ring, bearing the king's name and seal, on Joseph's finger, authorizing him to transact all of the kingdom's official business. Joseph was dressed in royal robes of fine linen, and the golden chain of the prime minister's office was placed about his neck. He rode in Pharaoh's chariot with men running before him shouting, "Make way! Make way!" Pharaoh said to Joseph, "I am Pharaoh, but without your word, no one can lift a hand or foot in all of Egypt."

The teenage slave who had arrived in Egypt was now the thirty-year-old prime minister of Egypt, the wealthiest and mightiest civilization on the face of the earth. Joseph came into Egypt bound in iron chains; now he wore the gold chains of royalty. In the past he had ridden on the back of a mangy camel into the slave market; now he rode in a royal chariot pulled by prancing stallions with heralds running before him, announcing the coming of Egypt's most-honored citizen.

Joseph had predicted seven years of prosperity and plenty, followed by seven years of famine. Under his leadership, the administration produced and banked surplus grain. Thus, when the years of famine came as predicted and the world ran out of food, Joseph, the Jewish ambassador who had been placed in a position of power by God, was able to barter with the nations of the earth until Egypt literally controlled the known world. As long as Pharaoh blessed Joseph and the Jews, Egypt's prosperity was so staggering that world historians struggle to accurately describe its splendor.

Egypt became the envy of the world. No nation on the earth had a fraction of her wealth, military power, or dazzling architectural beauty. Egypt prospered in personal health, international finance, and agricultural accomplishment.

"In thee shall all the nations of the earth be blessed." Joseph proved it.

Egypt Cursed Because of Joseph

After the years of prosperity Egypt enjoyed because of God's blessings, eventually a pharaoh who "knew not Joseph" (Exodus 1:8, KJV) came to power. As the memories of Joseph's remarkable leadership dimmed, the Egyptians began to persecute his descendants. They became slave labor for the pharaoh's expansive building projects. He made the lives of the Jewish people in Egypt grievous, first by working them ruthlessly hard, and finally by executing their sons by drowning them in the Nile River.

God raised up Moses as their leader, then sent ten plagues to crush Egypt. The firstborn in every Egyptian family died, all those who did not place lamb's blood over the doorpost. The nation's cattle lay dead in the fields, their grain was eaten by locusts, and the wealth of Egypt was given to the Jews as they left on that first Passover night. Finally, God drowned Pharaoh and his army in the Red Sea.

Egypt was bankrupt, facing starvation again because their cattle and grain were destroyed. Egypt was headless (the pharaoh was dead) and defenseless (the army was decimated). From that day until this, Egypt has gone from being the leader of the world to an emaciated, sick, and poverty-stricken society.

Why? "I will curse those who curse you..."

New Testament Gentiles Blessed
for Helping Jews

The principle that the Gentiles are blessed through the Jewish people is verified in the New Testament. Jesus Christ of Nazareth, a rabbi, was "a light to bring revelation to the Gentiles" (Luke 2:32).

When the Samaritan woman (a Gentile) went to the well to get water, Jesus said to her, "You [Gentiles] worship what you do not know; we [the Jews] know what we worship, for salvation is of the Jews" (John 4:22).

Luke's Gospel describes an occasion when Jesus went to Capernaum, where a certain Roman centurion (a Gentile) had a servant who was about to die. When the centurion heard that Jesus was coming, he sent Jewish elders to plead for Jesus to come and heal the critically ill servant.

Notice the logic the Jewish elders used with Jesus:

> And when they came to Jesus, they begged Him earnestly, saying that the one [the centurion] for whom He should do this was deserving, "for he *loves our nation [Israel], and has built us a synagogue.*" Then Jesus went with them.
>
> —Luke 7:4–6, emphasis added

The Jewish elders sought Jesus's help because this Roman soldier had blessed them by doing something practical for Israel—building a synagogue. So Jesus went to the house of a Gentile and healed the servant who was near death. Why? Because the Gentile had blessed the nation of Israel.

After the death and resurrection of Jesus, the same type of blessing was poured out on the Gentiles through the apostles. Scripture dramatically portrays what happened when the gospel was first preached to the Gentiles at the home of a man, another Roman centurion, living in the coastal city of Caesarea. Why did God select the household of Cornelius to be the first Gentiles to hear the gospel and to receive salvation and the outpouring of the Holy Spirit? The answer is recorded in Acts 10.

Cornelius is described in Scripture as "a devout man and one who feared God...*who gave alms generously to the people*" (Acts 10:2). Which people? The Jews who were living around him in Caesarea.

Scripture stresses that the reason God selected the residence of Cornelius for this great spiritual blessing was because he blessed the Jewish people:

> Cornelius, your prayer has been heard, and *your alms are remembered* in the sight of God.
>
> —Acts 10:31, emphasis added

Cornelius was selected because "he has a good reputation among all the nation of the Jews" (Acts 10:22). The point is made three times in the same chapter. A righteous Gentile who expressed his unconditional love for the Jewish people in a practical manner was divinely selected by heaven to be the first Gentile house to receive the gospel of salvation and the first to receive the outpouring of the Holy Spirit.

It was the practical acts of kindness on the part of a Gentile that provoked the blessing of God on his household, fulfilling the covenant made with Abraham: "I will bless those that bless you..."

The tragedy of history has been that for two thousand years, Christianity has not provoked Jews to jealousy by their kindness; instead, the church has produced a harvest of hatred that caused the Jewish people to recoil in fear from those who waged war beneath the cross. The perverted "Christianity" displayed by the Crusaders and Nazis is no different than a member of the Taliban who straps himself with a bomb and murders Jews who refuse to believe in Islam.

It's time for true Christians to reach out to our Jewish brothers and sisters, demonstrating the unconditional love of God, which is what Paul commanded in his letter to the Romans:

> For if the Gentiles have been partakers of their spiritual things [the Jews], their duty [the Gentiles] is also to minister to them [the Jewish people] in material things.
>
> —Romans 15:27

What "spiritual things" have the Gentiles received from the Jews? As Gentiles:

- We receive the unsearchable riches of the gospel of Jesus Christ.
- We receive the riches of the blessings of Abraham, which know no measure and have no limit.
- We receive the riches of faith by which the treasures of heaven are made possible to each of us.

- We receive the riches of repentance through which each of us becomes a child of God.
- We receive the riches of His love, joy, and eternal peace in the Holy Spirit.
- We receive the riches of salvation by grace through faith.
- We receive the riches of adoption and the riches of being heirs and joint heirs with Jesus Christ.

We have received the Word of God from the Jewish people. We have received the patriarchs and the prophets. We have received a monotheistic theology; that is, one God, the God of Abraham, Isaac, and Jacob. Tragically, most Christians do not understand how blessed we are because of the Jewish people.

In fact, far too many Christians labor under theological misconceptions about the relationship of Judaism and Christianity. In the next chapter I will lay to rest some of the myths and errors that have driven these two great, biblically connected faiths apart.

CHAPTER 10

ANSWERING CHRISTIAN CRITICS

OVER THE YEARS, MY UNWAVERING SUPPORT FOR THE State of Israel and my outreach to the Jewish community has been misunderstood and mischaracterized by Christian and secular critics alike. In this chapter and the next, I want to respond to some of the most frequent criticisms I receive, clarify my position, and make my final points in the case for supporting the Jewish state.

I will begin by repeating some of the common misperceptions about Jesus and the Jewish people, especially by those who teach the error of replacement theology, the idea that the church has replaced the nation of Israel and the Jews in the economy of God. This false doctrine holds that the historic nation of Israel no longer has a part in God's divine plan for the remainder of time. Replacement theology is the underpinning of most of the atrocities committed in the name of Christianity against the Jewish people over the centuries.

Many Christians have never even heard the term *replacement theology* and are unaware that they have fallen prey to doctrinal error. These people may raise some of the following objections without realizing the implication of their statements.

The Jews Are Not Christ Killers

Early church fathers told their illiterate congregants that the Jews were the odious assassins of Christ. Century after century this vicious label was tied about the necks of the Jews, and as a result, the Crusaders, the Inquisitors, and the Nazis turned Europe red with Jewish blood—all believing they were acting in accordance with God's will.

The early church historian Eusebius, in the first paragraph of *Church History*, declared that it was his intention to "recount the misfortunes which immediately came upon *the whole Jewish nation* in consequence of their plots against the Savior."[1]

St. Gregory of Nyssa mounted his pulpit, ranting against Jews as the "*slayers of the Lord*, murderers of the prophets, adversaries of God, haters of God, men who show contempt for the law, foes of grace, enemies of their fathers' faith, advocates of the devil, brood of vipers, slanderers, scoffers, men whose minds are in darkness, leaven of the Pharisees, assembly of demons, sinners, wicked men, stoners and haters of righteousness."[2]

St. John Chrysostom coined the term *deicide Jews* ("killers of Christ"). It was a vicious label the Jews were never able to escape. This Roman church leader's anti-Semitic teachings were recorded in his homilies:

The Jews are the most worthless of all men. They are lech-
erous, greedy, rapacious. They are perfidious *murderers
of Christ*. They worship the devil, their religion is a sick-
ness. The Jews are the *odious assassins of Christ and for
killing God* there is no expiation possible, no indulgence
or pardon. Christians may never cease vengeance, and the
Jew must live in servitude forever. God always hated the
Jews, it is incumbent upon all Christians (i.e., their duty)
to hate the Jews.[3]

The Nazis prepared the German people for the extermination of
the Jews by exploiting this crucifixion theme with its corollary of
unending divine judgment. The "Christ killers" label motivated the
German people to be silent and turn their heads while the Nazis
marched the apple of God's eye toward mass extermination ditches
and finally into the ovens.

How could this madness happen at the hands of one of the
most civilized and cultured peoples on the earth? How could it be
justified in the minds of the Christian-baptized German people? It
was done with the oft-repeated poisonous phrase: "The Jews are the
Christ killers!"

Hermann Grabe was an eyewitness to what happened at Dulmo,
in Ukraine, as a result of years of religious rhetoric blaming the
Jews for the crucifixion of Jesus Christ.

On October 5, 1942, Grabe went to his office in Dulmo, where
he was told by his foreman that all the Jews in the neighborhood
were being exterminated. About fifteen hundred were being shot
each day in massive extermination ditches. Grabe and his foreman

got into a car and drove to the execution ditches the Nazis had prepared, thirty meters long and three meters deep. As they arrived, they saw the Nazi SS using dogs and whips to drive the Jews off the packed trucks toward the massive extermination ditches.

> The Jews were ordered to strip. They were told to put down their clothes in tidy order, boots and shoes, top clothing and underclothing. Already there were great piles of this clothing and a heap of eight hundred to a thousand pairs of boots and shoes.[4]

The people undressed. The mothers undressed their little children "without screaming or weeping," reported Grabe, five years afterward. They had reached a point of human suffering where tears no longer flow and all hope has been abandoned. "They stood around in family groups, kissed each other, said farewells, and waited."

They were waiting for a signal from the SS man, who was standing by the pit holding his whip. They stood there waiting for a quarter of an hour, waiting for their turn to come, while on the other side of the earth mound, now that the shots were no longer heard, the dead and the dying were being packed into the pit.

Grabe said:

> I heard no complaints, no appeal for mercy. I watched a family of about eight persons, a man and a woman both about fifty, with their grownup children, about twenty to twenty-four. An old woman with snow-white hair was holding a little baby in her arms, singing to it and tickling it. The baby was cooing with delight. The couple were

looking at each other with tears in their eyes. The father was holding the hand of a boy about ten years old and speaking to him softly; the boy was fighting his tears....

They were marched into the execution ditch and shot in the usual Nazi fashion in the back of the head. Dr. James Parkes writes, "In our day...more than six million deliberate murders are the consequences of the teachings about Jews for which the Christian Church is ultimately responsible...which has its ultimate resting place in the teaching of the New Testament itself."[5]

One of those deadly New Testament myths is that the Jews killed Jesus, yet no justification can be found in the New Testament to support this lie. When you are confronted with this misstatement about the Jewish people, here are a few things that you can mention in your response.

First of all, in any court trial, eyewitness accounts are considered the only acceptable source of testimony in the pursuit of truth. What do the eyewitness accounts in the Gospels have to say? The writers of the Gospels took special care to impress upon their readers the fact that the Jewish people, their own people, were not responsible for, and were for the most part ignorant of, the events that led up to the arrest, trial, and conviction of Jesus Christ.

The Eyewitness Accounts

Matthew states that the Jews as a people had nothing to do with the political conspiracy against Jesus. The conspirators are exposed in this way:

> Then the chief priests and the elders of the people assembled in the palace of the high priest, whose name was Caiaphas, and *they plotted* to arrest Jesus in some sly way and kill him.
>
> —Matthew 26:3–4, NIV, emphasis added

> And the scribes and chief priests heard it and sought how they might destroy Him; for they feared Him, because *all the people* were astonished at His teaching.
>
> —Mark 11:18, emphasis added

> And the chief priests and the scribes sought how they might kill Him, for *they feared the people.*
>
> —Luke 22:2, emphasis added

Two very important points must be made here:

1. There was a crucifixion plot.
2. It was carried out by the high priest Caiaphas, who did not in any way represent the Jewish people. He was a political appointment of Herod, who was himself directly appointed by Rome, not the Jewish people. The Jewish people hated Herod and Caiaphas because they were political pawns in the hands of the pagan Romans.

How did Herod come to power? Forty years before Christ was born, Mark Anthony of Rome joined military forces with Herod the Great in an attack on the city of Jerusalem. After five months, Jerusalem fell, and Herod was appointed by Mark Anthony as the

Roman supervisor of Palestine. Herod was a dictator and a paranoid murderer from whom Hitler could have learned a few lessons.

Herod promptly had forty-five members of the *Sanhedrin*, the ancient Jewish equivalent of a Supreme Court, murdered to gain absolute dictatorial control and silence the Jewish voice in government. During the reign of Herod, the Sanhedrin was nothing more than a powerless religious court. Herod now had absolute power by the will of Rome, not the Jewish people.

Caiaphas, who led the "Calvary Plot," was appointed by Herod to do the will of Rome. He was an illegitimate priest who was not selected by the Jewish people to do their will. The high priest was a political pawn who was despised by the Jews of Jerusalem.

Into this political setting walked a Jewish rabbi named Jesus of Nazareth. The Jews were looking for a deliverer who would lead a revolt to break the oppressive chains of Rome. The popularity of Jesus spread like chained lightning. Anyone who could feed five thousand people out of one boy's sack lunch could feed an army that could defeat Rome. Anyone who could heal and raise people from the dead could heal wounded soldiers and raise dead troops back to life to fight the pagan Romans.

Jesus Christ was a very serious political threat to Herod and to his stooge, Caiaphas. So they entered into a politically inspired plot to have Jesus killed Roman style: by crucifixion. When Rome's co-conspirator, the high priest Caiaphas, met with his political rogues to consider how to kill Jesus of Nazareth, the biblical text states that they determined to arrest Jesus in a sly way lest they cause a riot among the Jewish people.

And they plotted to arrest Jesus in some sly way and kill him. "But not during the Feast [Passover]," they said, "or there may be a *riot among the people.*"

—Matthew 26:4–5, NIV, emphasis added

And they sought to lay hands on Him, but *feared the multitude.*

—Mark 12:12, emphasis added

But they said, "Not during the feast, lest there be an *uproar of the people.*"

—Mark 14:2, emphasis added

Why did they fear a riot? A riot requires the *spontaneous uprising* among the general population. The high priest knew that the majority of the people supported Jesus and would spontaneously riot if he were captured. News of a riot would get back to Rome, and Herod would be instantly replaced from his very lucrative position. If Herod lost his political power, so would Caiaphas. They could not let that happen, so they derived a plot.

Matthew contributes more evidence that the leaders of this plot *feared the Jewish people* if they abused Jesus.

They looked for a way to arrest him, but they were *afraid of the crowd* because the people held that he was a prophet.

—Matthew 21:46, NIV, emphasis added

The high priest and his circle of religious conspirators had no mandate from the people; rather, they feared the people. They most certainly did not represent the one million Jews who were living in Palestine at the time, much less the millions of Jews who lived in Egypt or were scattered over the Roman Empire. These religious rogues were a miniscule handful, led by the high priest to do Rome's bidding.

But what about the mob who screamed, "His blood be on us and on our children" (Matthew 27:25)? Some have used this as scriptural proof that all the Jewish people on the earth are forever guilty of the blood of Jesus Christ and deserve eternal punishment from the Almighty. Not so!

The truth is that the political puppet, Caiaphas, is the one who *gathered and controlled the crowd*. Remember, this was an orchestrated plot, not a spontaneous expression of the people. The apostle Matthew, an eyewitness, says:

> But the chief priests and the elders *persuaded the crowd* to ask for Barabbas and to have Jesus executed.
>
> —Matthew 27:20, NIV, emphasis added

How did they persuade the crowd? The Pharisees in the school of Hillel were as mad as hornets because Jesus would not endorse Shammai's teaching on "divorce for every cause." It took no oratorical gift to get a group of them to scream for the crucifixion of Jesus. They could not have numbered more than a few hundred, and they were more than glad to do it.

When the crucified Jesus arose from the dead after three days, it meant big problems for the local theologians. The moral corruption of Caiaphas once again manifested itself. He gave large political bribes to the military guards watching the tomb, telling them to lie about what had happened. From the eyewitness account we read:

> When the chief priests had met with the elders and *devised a plan*, they gave the soldiers a *large sum of money*, telling them, "*You are to say*, 'His disciples came during the night and stole him away while we were asleep.' If this report gets to the governor, *we will satisfy him* and keep you out of trouble."
>
> —Matthew 28:12–14, NIV, emphasis added

There are five points that must not be missed in this important verse:

1. The chief priest was a conspirator.

2. He was guilty of offering a Roman soldier a political bribe, which was a criminal act punishable by death.

3. He was a liar who paid other people to lie.

4. The Roman soldier could have been put to death for sleeping at his post, but the chief priest was so confident of his political connection to the Roman governor that he promised to "satisfy him" and assured the soldier that he would "keep him out of trouble."

5. The fact that the chief priest was politically connected was common public knowledge, or else the Roman soldier would never have placed his life in jeopardy by

accepting the bribe and becoming a part of this religious plot.

Consider also that Jesus himself identified his killers:

> Then He took the twelve aside and said to them, "Behold, we are going up to Jerusalem, and all things that are written by the prophets concerning the Son of Man will be accomplished. For He will be *delivered to the Gentiles* [the Romans] and will be mocked and insulted and spit upon. They will scourge Him and *kill Him*. And the third day He will rise again."
>
> —Luke 18:31–33, emphasis added

The biblical text is perfectly clear: Jesus was crucified by Rome as a political insurrectionist who was considered too dangerous to live. He was a threat to Herod's grip on Palestine and a threat to the high priest. The plot among Herod's inner circle produced the Roman crucifixion of Jesus Christ at Calvary. It had nothing to do with the Jewish people as a civilization.

The historical fact is that three out of four Jews did not live in what the Romans called Palestine when Jesus began his ministry. Nine out of ten of the Jews in Palestine at that time lived outside of Jerusalem. Only a few hundred irate Pharisees could have possibly participated in the plot led by the high priest.

The justice of God would never permit judgment for the sins of a handful of people to be passed to an entire civilization of people. In the last breath of his earthly life, Jesus forgave even the high priest and his conspirators with, "Father, forgive them, for they do not know what they do" (Luke 23:34).

If God has forgiven, why can't Christians?

The Jews Did Not Reject Jesus as Messiah

Most evangelicals believe the Jews rejected Jesus as Messiah and therefore qualify for God's eternal judgment. Replacement theologians have said that "the covenant with Israel was broken because she *would not accept Jesus Christ whom God sent*."[6]

Is this statement about the Jewish people biblically true? No! In order to respond to this misstatement about the Jews, several questions must be answered:

- Did the Jews reject Jesus as Messiah, or did Jesus refuse to be their Messiah?

- Did the words of Jesus or his actions convey the message that he wanted to be Messiah?

- Did the Jews want Jesus to be their Messiah?

- What does the biblical text say was the sovereign plan of God for the life of Jesus Christ?

God's Sovereign Will for Jesus

Anyone who reads the Bible knows that almighty God has a sovereign will that no man or nation can change or control. That is also true about the life of Jesus Christ. What was God's sovereign will for his life as recorded in Scripture?

When Jesus was still an infant, the Holy Spirit spoke through Simeon concerning God's sovereign will for the life of Jesus:

> So he [Simeon] came by the Spirit into the temple. And when the parents brought in the Child Jesus, to do for Him according to the custom of the law, he took Him up in his arms and blessed God and said: "Lord, now You are letting Your servant depart in peace, according to Your word; for mine eyes have seen Your salvation which You have prepared before the face of all peoples, *a light to bring revelation to the Gentiles*, and the glory of Your people Israel.
>
> —Luke 2:27–32, emphasis added

The Holy Spirit of God announced through a Jewish prophet, Simeon, that the sovereign purpose for Jesus's life was to be a *light to the Gentiles* (compare Isaiah 42:6).

This was a shocking revelation, because the Jews considered the Gentiles unclean; they were "aliens from the commonwealth of Israel and strangers from the covenants of promise, having no hope and without God in the world" (Ephesians 2:12).

The prejudice of the disciples against the "unclean" polytheistic Gentiles was so strong that it took a divine rebuke from the angel of the Lord to get Peter to share the gospel with the Gentiles in the home of Cornelius (Acts 10:9–16). When Peter saw the sheet (which I believe was actually a prayer shawl) let down from heaven by its four corners and saw it full of "unclean creatures," he was repulsed.

That's why the Great Commission commanded, "Go ye [Jews] into all the world and preach the gospel to every creature..." Gentiles were considered creatures. Jesus even referred to the Gentiles as dogs. The message of the gospel was from Israel, not to Israel! When Peter obeyed the Lord and went to the house of Cornelius, the Jewish church was enraged that he would do such an unthinkable thing (Acts 15; Galatians 2).

John the Baptist Speaks

John the Baptist said to his listeners as Jesus came to the Jordan River to be baptized, "Behold! The *Lamb of God* who takes away the sin of the world!" (John 1:29).

Every Jewish person who heard John's words knew there was only one thing you could do with a young male lamb: kill it! John the Baptist was stating that the primary purpose for Jesus's life was the cross, not a crown. He spoke of Jesus's death, not his diadem.

John the Revelator describes Jesus as "the Lamb slain from the foundation of the world" (Revelation 13:8). It was God's sovereign will for Jesus to die from the very dawning of time. Had Jesus permitted himself to become the reigning Messiah to the Jews, he would have missed the sovereign will of God for his life.

The Crisis Theory

Replacement theologians have created a crisis theory as the catch-22 of the New Testament. The crisis theory goes like this: "God had Plan A and Plan B for the ministry of Jesus Christ while he was on earth. Plan A was for Jesus to be the Messiah of Israel. Plan B was the cross of Calvary. Since the Jews rejected Jesus as Messiah, God had no choice but to go to Plan B, the crucifixion."

This is utter rubbish! First, it makes a sovereign and almighty God subject to the whims and choices of man.

Second, the biblical text parades three witness before us (Simeon, John the Baptist, and John the Revelator) who plainly state that God's plan from the beginning was for Jesus to die. Had Jesus not gone to the cross, not one Gentile would have ever come to redemption.

"I've Come to Die!"

When Jesus spoke to Nicodemus he said, "And as Moses lifted up the serpent in the wilderness, even so must the Son of Man be lifted up" (John 3:14). This is a clear reference to his death on the cross.

When Mary of Bethany came and anointed the feet of Jesus, he said, "She has come beforehand to anoint My body for burial" (Mark 14:8). Jesus told his disciples, "Thus it is written, and thus it was necessary for the Christ to suffer and to rise from the dead the third day" (Luke 24:46). It is obvious from the biblical text that God's will for Jesus was to die on the cross and that Jesus carried out that assignment with joy (Hebrews 12:2).

Five major points must now be made that are crucial to understanding that the Jews did not reject Jesus as Messiah.

1. Jesus had to live to be the Messiah.
2. If it was God's will for Jesus to die from the beginning...

135

3. If it was Jesus intention to be obedient unto death...

4. If there is not one verse of Scripture in the New Testament that says Jesus came to be the Messiah...

5. And if Jesus refused by his words or actions to claim to be the Messiah to the Jews, then *how can the Jews be blamed for rejecting what was never offered?*

"Give Us a Sign!"

The Jews were accustomed to their leaders demonstrating their call from God with supernatural signs. When God called Moses from the backside of the desert to go into Egypt and lead millions of Hebrew slaves out of bondage, God gave Moses four signs to convince the children of Israel that he was their *messiah.*

The first sign that God gave to Moses was for Moses himself to verify that he was indeed God's anointed. God commanded Moses to throw his shepherd's rod down on the ground, and it became a snake, causing Moses to flee from it. Any nagging doubts Moses might have had vanished! He knew he was anointed of God to overthrow Egypt and lead the Jewish people to the Promised Land.

The next two signs God gave Moses were to convince the children of Israel that Moses was their messiah. God told Moses to put his hand in his bosom. He did, and it instantly became white with leprosy. God ordered Moses to put his hand in his bosom a second time. He did, and his hand was restored "like his other flesh" (Exodus 4:7).

God continued his instructions to Moses by saying, "If they do not believe you, nor heed the message of the first sign, that they may believe the message of the latter sign" (verse 8). The Jews had been in slavery more than four hundred years, and it was imperative to the sovereign plan of God that the Jews recognize Moses as their messiah.

For this reason God gave Moses a fourth sign that would convince the most skeptical Jewish slave in Egypt.

> And it shall be, if they do not believe even these two signs, or listen to your voice, that you shall take water from the river and pour it on the dry land. The water which you take from the river will become blood on the dry land.
>
> —Exodus 4:9

Moses used these four signs to convince the children of Israel, who had been in slavery for four hundred years, that he was God's anointed leader or messiah.

If God intended for Jesus to be the Messiah of Israel, why didn't he authorize Jesus to use supernatural signs to prove he was God's Messiah, just as Moses had done? The Jews, knowing of Moses's signs to Israel, asked for a supernatural sign that Jesus was indeed their Messiah. Jesus answered:

> No sign will be given...except the sign of the prophet Jonah. For as Jonah was three days and three nights in the belly of the great fish, so will the Son of Man be three days and three nights in the heart of the earth.
>
> —Matthew 12:39–40

Jesus refused to give a sign. He only compared himself to the prophet Jonah, who carried the message of repentance from God to the Gentiles at Nineveh. Jesus was again saying, "I have come to carry a message from God to the Gentiles and will be in my grave for three days and nights as Jonah was in the whale's belly for three days and nights."

Jesus gave Peter, sometimes called Simon Peter (or just Simon), a commission to the Gentiles with the words, "Blessed are you, Simon Bar-Jonah" (Matthew 16:17). He was not referring to Simon's father but to the prophet Jonah, who, as a Jew, reluctantly carried God's message to the Ninevites, who were Gentiles.

Peter was the Jewish messenger who would, as Jonah, carry the gospel message to the Gentiles in the house of Cornelius. When the angel of the Lord found Peter, he was on a rooftop in Joppa, the same city where Jonah had fled to avoid going to Nineveh. Both men went from Joppa to the Gentiles, both men were forced of God to go, and both were extremely successful.

Herod Asked for a Sign

When Jesus went on trial, Herod "had desired for a long time to see Him...and he hoped to see some miracle [sign] done by Him" (Luke 23:8). Jesus refused to produce a sign for the national leadership of Israel in an attempt to prove he was the Messiah because it was not the Father's will, nor his, to be Messiah. Jesus's repeated response to the Jewish people who urged him to be their Messiah was, "My kingdom is not of this world" (John 18:36).

"Tell No One!"

If Jesus wanted to be Messiah, why did he repeatedly tell his disciples and followers to "tell no one" about his supernatural accomplishments? Think about it! If the man were trying to gain national attention to rally the support of the general public for the overthrow of mighty Rome, he would not go around the country saying, "Tell no one!"

He would have conducted himself like any other politician who would do anything the mind of man could imagine to make the nightly news. The name of the game is to create public awareness. Let people know who you are and what you propose to do.

What did Jesus do?

There are sixty-four occasions in the four Gospels where Jesus threw a wet blanket over his popularity by instructing those who were excited about his being Messiah to "tell no one." The people wanted him to be their Messiah, but he absolutely refused.

When Jesus healed the leper, he instructed him, "See that you tell no one" (Matthew 8:1–4). When he cast evil spirits out of the multitudes that followed him and they cried out saying, "You are the Son of God," Jesus would not allow them to speak, for "they knew that He was the Christ" (Luke 4:41). When he raised Jairus's daughter from the dead, he charged the parents of the dead girl "to tell no one what had happened" (Luke 8:56). When he opened deaf ears, "He commanded them that they should tell no one" (Mark 7:36). When he healed the blind man at Bethsaida by spitting on his eye, he ordered him, saying, "Neither go into the town, nor tell anyone in the town" (Mark 8:26). When Jesus healed two blind men in Matthew 9, he "sternly warned them, saying, 'See that no one knows it'" (verse 30).

When impetuous Peter could stand it no longer, he blurted out, "You are the Christ." Or in other words, "You are the anointed one! You are the Messiah who will lead the Jews in their revolt against Rome." But Jesus strictly warned his disciples "that they should tell no one about Him" (Mark 8:29–30).

After the transfiguration, where the disciples had heard Moses talking to Jesus and the voice of God spoke from the cloud, saying, "This is My beloved Son," Jesus commanded his disciples as they were coming down the mountain to "tell no one the things they had seen, till the Son of Man had risen from the dead" (Mark 9:1–9).

Why did he constantly command those who were excited about his supernatural abilities to "tell no one"? The Jews were not rejecting Jesus as Messiah; it was Jesus who was refusing to be the Messiah to the Jews.

Jews for Jesus

There were many "Jews for Jesus" when Christ fed five thousand men and their families with two biscuits and five sardines. Anyone who could feed that many people with so little could feed an army that could fight Rome. Anyone who could heal leprosy could heal a soldier wounded in combat. Anyone who could raise Lazarus from the dead could raise a dead soldier who fought in his army. This Nazarene had something going for him that Rome couldn't match. Make no mistake about it, there were multiplied thousands of Jews for Jesus while he was walking on water, feeding the masses, and raising the dead.

He performed these miracles to minister to the needs of people; they were not intended to be a demonstration of supernatural signs to prove he was the Messiah. Every miracle Jesus did for the people they had seen before in the Old Testament. The signs that Moses used to verify he was indeed God's leader for Israel had never been seen before.

The multiplied thousands who followed Jesus did not give up the idea that he would be their Messiah until they saw him hanging from a Roman cross. Even after his resurrection and his repeated denials that he would not be the Messiah, his disciples were still hanging on to the last thread of hope that he would now smash Rome (Acts 1:6). They wanted him to be their Messiah, but he flatly refused.

The Pushy Mother

The mother of James and John wanted Jesus to be Messiah. Right up until the shadow of his cross fell across the bloody sands of Calvary, the mother of James and John put on a full-court press, trying to get Jesus to agree to place her two sons at his right hand and at his left hand whenever he entered his kingdom (Matthew 20:20–28).

She was not thinking about a Roman cross; she was thinking about positions of influence and power for her sons in an earthly political kingdom. When Jesus defeated Rome as the Jewish Messiah, ushering in an era of universal peace, she wanted her sons in positions of power.

What was Jesus's response?

He looked at this presumptuous Jewish mother and said, "You don't know what you're asking for your two sons. I didn't come to be served [to rule]; I came to die!"

Two Disciples on the Emmaus Road

The two disciples on the road to Emmaus (located seven miles outside Jerusalem) wanted Jesus to be the Messiah. Luke mentions one of them by name: Cleopas, the father of James the Less. The other disciple walking on the road with him may have been his wife, Mary. As they walked, Jesus himself joined them, but they did not recognize him.

> He asked them, "What are you discussing together as you walk along?"
>
> …One of them, named Cleopas asked him, "Are you only a visitor to Jerusalem and do not know the things that have happened there in these days?
>
> "What things?" he asked.
>
> "About Jesus of Nazareth," they replied. "He was a prophet, powerful in word and deed before God and all the people. The chief priests and our rulers handed him over to be sentenced to death, and they crucified him; *but we had hoped that he was the one who was going to redeem Israel.*"
>
> —Luke 24:17–21, NIV, emphasis added

The two disciples on the road to Emmaus had not rejected Jesus as Messiah; their hopes were dashed!

It was not until Jesus entered their house for fellowship, as it was late in the evening, that they recognized him. When he sat at their table, lifting his hands to bless and break the bread, they saw the scars on his hands and recognized Jesus. He instantly disappeared (Luke 24:30–35). He refused to be their Messiah, choosing instead to be the Savior of the world.

The Last Supper

Christians have little understanding of our Jewish roots and become confused when discussing the Last Supper and the Passover. Most think they are one and the same. They are not.

There are four days of preparation for Passover, beginning at the tenth of Nisan. At sunset on the tenth of the month, a series of three evening meals begin, all of which are served with leavened bread and fermented foods.

The first meal on the tenth of the month is called the "Feast of the First Night." The second meal served on the eleventh of the month is called the "Feast of the Second Night." The third meal, which is served on the twelfth of the month, is called the "Feast of the Third Night." The next night, on the thirteenth of the month at sunset, the last meal with leavened bread and fermented foods was eaten before Passover, which was the following evening, the fourteenth of Nisan or April. The last meal where leavened bread and fermented foods could be served was called the Last Supper. It is the night before Passover and is separate in purpose and meaning.

The apostle John describes Jesus dipping leavened bread that Judas took before leaving the Last Supper to betray the Lord. While the other Gospels mention articles of Passover, John verifies that the betrayal took place at the time of the Last Supper. It could not have been Passover, because the high priest who paid thirty pieces of silver to Judas would never have executed any kind of economic transaction on such a holy day.

After the eating of the Last Supper at which he was betrayed, Jesus celebrated the Passover the next evening at sundown with his disciples, minus Judas. It was here that he uniquely rejects for the final time the messiahship of Israel.

It has been my privilege to join Congregation Rodfei Sholom in San Antonio for the celebration of Passover with Rabbi Aryeh Scheinberg. Four cups of wine are served at the Passover with a meal that symbolized the tears and suffering of the Hebrew slaves in Egypt.

- The first cup is the cup of Remembrance.
- The second cup is the cup of Redemption.
- The third cup is the cup of Salvation.
- The fourth cup is the cup of Messiah.

When Jesus and his disciples came to the final cup during their last celebration of the Passover, *Jesus refused to drink* the Messiah's cup. He told his disciples, "Take this [Messiah's cup] and divide it among yourselves; for I say to you, I will not drink of the fruit of the vine until the kingdom of God comes" (Luke 22:17–18).

In refusing to drink the cup, Jesus rejected to the last detail the role of Messiah in word or deed. The Jews did not reject Jesus as Messiah; it was Jesus who rejected the Jewish desire for him to be their Messiah.

The Church Has Not Replaced Israel

Replacement theologians teach that God is finished with Israel. In their view, Israel has been rejected and replaced by the church to carry out the work once entrusted to Israel. The Jewish people have ceased to be God's people, and the church is now spiritual Israel.

This misconception is rooted in the theological anti-Semitism that began in the first century. As I said before, the early Christians who received the Great Commission to go into all the world and preach the gospel "to every creature" were Jewish. The "creatures" were the unclean Gentiles.

The apostle Paul clearly states that before the Jews brought the gospel to the Gentiles, the Gentiles walked in total spiritual darkness.

> At that time you were without Christ, being aliens from the commonwealth of Israel and strangers from the covenants of promise, having no hope and without God in the world. But now in Christ Jesus you who once were far off have been brought near by the blood of Christ. For He Himself is our peace, who has made both one, and has broken down the middle wall of separation.
>
> —Ephesians 2:12–14

The teaching that "the church is the new Israel" originated in the first century because the Gentile converts resented the priority of the Jewish people in the economy of God. Arrogance and pride cause this theology of hate to flourish today. It appeals to the ego to say, "We are the only people of God!"

Replacement theology is not a new revelation; it's an old heresy. The author of the *Epistles* of Ignatius of Antioch (ca. 70–107) presents the church as "the new Israel." He also portrays the prophets and heroes of Israel as "Christians before their time" and not part of the Jewish religion.

Those who teach that the church is the new Israel must use the *allegorical* method of interpreting Scripture. It is not possible to examine the *literal, historical* statements of the biblical text and conclude that God is finished with Israel and the church has taken her place.

Scripture plainly indicates that the church (spiritual Israel) and national Israel exist side by side, and neither replaces the other— *ever*! Here are some ways to respond when people try to tell you that Christians and the church have replaced the Jews.

"Comfort Ye My People"

There are two Israels in Scripture. One is a physical Israel, with a physical people, a physical Jerusalem, and physical borders that are plainly defined in Scripture. There is also a spiritual Israel, with a spiritual people and a spiritual New Jerusalem. Spiritual Israel (the church) may have the blessings of physical Israel, but it does not replace physical Israel in the economy of God.

This is clearly seen in Isaiah 40:1 which states; "*Comfort ye, comfort ye my people,* saith your God" (KJV, emphasis added).

The question must be asked, "Who is the 'ye' of this verse?" It's plural, so it is not one person; it is a body of people. "My people" is also plural. There are, in fact, two groups of people in this verse. One group is being comforted, and the other is the comforter.

Common logic will tell you that you cannot be the one who is *being comforted* and also be *the comforter.* The people being comforted in this verse are "my people," which is physical Israel. The one doing the comforting (instructed to "comfort ye") is spiritual Israel, the church. These two Israels will merge together not one day sooner than the moment when the Messiah literally comes to the physical city of Jerusalem.

Replacement theologians in America are preaching "that if Christians will quit supporting Israel and will economically boycott the Christ-rejecting Jews, they will accept Jesus Christ."[7] In addition to causing a regression back to the quality of life of the Dark Ages, an economic boycott of Israel is not going to result in a massive conversion of Jews. This anti-Semitic logic defies and ignores both history and the Bible.

The Crusaders economically attacked the Jews and robbed them of their last dime in the name of God. The Jews did not become Christians. The leaders of the Spanish Inquisition robbed the Jews of their wealth while the Roman church and state split the plunder. The Jews did not become Christians. Adolf Hitler brought economic ruin to the Jews by forbidding them to have jobs, destroying their places of businesses in the infamous Kristallnacht, and then fining them billions of marks to repair the damage his Nazi hoodlums inflicted. The Jews did not become Christians. Six million of them were systematically slaughtered, and as they walked to the gas chamber, they sang "Hatikvah," not "Amazing Grace"! They did not become Christians.

It is time for Christians everywhere to recognize that the nation of Israel will never convert to Christianity and join the Baptist church in their town.

- Yes, all Israel will be saved (Romans 11:26).
- Yes, Israel will look on the Messiah and accept him (Zechariah 12:10).
- Yes, Israel will be forgiven of all sin (Romans 11:27).

But the idea that the Jews of the world are going to convert and storm the doors of Christian churches is a myth. After two thousand years of a loveless, godless, anti-Semitic Christianity that has saturated the soil of the earth with their blood in the Crusades, the Inquisition, and the Holocaust, they are not about to convert. After two thousand years of an anti-Semitic replacement theology that says "the church is the real Israel," thus denying the Jews their rightful place in the economy of God, they are not about to convert.

Where is the Christianity that says, "Love thy neighbor as thyself"? Where is the Christianity that says, "Love does its neighbor no ill"? Where is the Christianity that follows the admonition of Christ to "love one another as I have loved you"? It is not Jews and Judaism who have lost credibility; it is a loveless Christianity that has lost credibility. The Jews ask, "Was Jesus a false messiah?" No one can be the true Messiah whose followers feel compelled to hate, murder, rob, and rape for two thousand years and then brazenly proclaim, "We are the people of God."

Sincere rabbis have asked me, "If Jesus is the real Messiah, the prince of peace, why are Christians always fighting each other?" I have no intelligent answer.

If Replaced, Why Reborn?

For eighteen hundred years Christian leaders ranted that "the church is the new Israel." To prove that God had turned his back on the Jews, they pointed to the wandering, tormented Jews of the Diaspora saying, "If God is with them, why has this befallen them?"

Forget that the Jews were living for the most part in papal states controlled by the church of Rome. They lived without rights, without property, without legal redress, and without human dignity in an environment created by the laws of the Roman church.

Replacement theologians ignore a fundamental fact in the biblical text. When God replaces something, *you never hear from it again.* It is twice dead, plucked up by the roots, and cast over the wall to be burned and forever forgotten. God destroyed Sodom and Gomorrah, and they have never been rediscovered.

On May 15, 1948, a theological earthquake leveled replacement theology when national Israel was reborn after nearly two millennia of wandering. From the four corners of the earth the seed of Abraham began to return to the land of their fathers. They returned "from their Gentile graves," speaking sixty different languages, and founded a nation that became a superpower in a few decades. Israel is not passing away; it's building, growing, inventing, and developing. The desert is blooming like the rose, just as the prophets of Israel promised.

If God was indeed finished with the Jews and Israel, if they were in truth a cast-off relic of the past without divine purpose or destiny, why did he allow that nation to be miraculously reborn? If replaced, why reborn?

Their rebirth was living, prophetic proof that Israel has not been replaced. They were "reborn in a day" (Isaiah 66:8) to form the Third Commonwealth of Israel, which shall endure until the coming of Messiah.

The Prophets Rebut Replacement Theology

If Israel as a nation had not been reborn, if the Jews had not returned to the land, if the cities of Israel had not been rebuilt, if Judea and Samaria (the West Bank) had not been occupied, if the trees that the Turks cut down had not been replanted, if the agricultural accomplishments of Israel had not been miraculous, there would be a valid reason for every person to doubt that the Word of God is true. But listen to the prophets of God declare his intention for the Jews of the world to reinhabit Israel.

Isaiah speaks

> Fear not, for I am with you; I will bring your descendants from the east, and gather you from the west; I will say to the north, "Give them up!" And to the south, "Do not keep them back!" Bring My sons from afar, and My daughters from the ends of the earth.
>
> —Isaiah 43:5–6

The ransomed of the LORD shall return, and come to Zion [Jerusalem] with singing, with everlasting joy on their heads. They shall obtain joy and gladness, and sorrow and sighing shall flee away.

—Isaiah 35:10

They shall rebuild the old ruins, they shall raise up the former desolations, and they shall repair the ruined cities, the desolation of many generations.

—Isaiah 61:4

I am the LORD...who says to Jerusalem, "You shall be inhabited," to the cities of Judah, "You shall be built," and I will raise up her waste places.

—Isaiah 44:24, 26

Ezekiel speaks

Thus says the Lord GOD: "When I have gathered the house of Israel from the peoples among whom they are scattered, and am hallowed in them in the sight of the Gentiles, then they will dwell in their own land which I gave to My servant Jacob. And they will dwell safely there, build houses, and plant vineyards; yes, they will dwell securely, when I execute judgments on all those around them who despise them. Then they shall know that I am the LORD their God."

—Ezekiel 28:25–26

"And they shall no longer be a prey for the nations, nor shall beasts of the land devour them; but they shall dwell safely, and no one shall make them afraid. I will raise up for them a garden of renown, and they shall no longer be consumed with hunger in the land, nor bear the shame of the Gentiles anymore. Thus they shall know that I, the LORD their God, am with them, and that they, the house of Israel, are My people," says the Lord GOD.

—Ezekiel 34:28–30

I will gather you from the peoples, assemble you from the countries where you have been scattered, and I will give you the land of Israel....I will give them one heart, and I will put a new spirit within them.

—Ezekiel 11:17, 19

Thus says the Lord GOD: "Surely I will take the children of Israel from among the nations, wherever they have gone, and will gather them from every side and bring them into their own land; and I will make them one nation in the land, on the mountains of Israel; and one king shall be king over them all; they shall no longer be two nations, nor shall they ever be divided into two kingdoms again. They shall not defile themselves anymore with their idols, nor with their detestable things, nor with any of their transgressions; but I will deliver them from all their dwelling places in which they have sinned, and will cleanse them. Then they shall be My people, and I will be their God.

David My servant shall be king over them, and they shall all have one shepherd; they shall also walk in My judgments and observe My statutes, and do them. Then they shall dwell in the land that I have given to Jacob My servant, where your fathers dwelt; and they shall dwell there, they, their children, and their children's children, forever; and My servant David shall be their prince forever. Moreover I will make a covenant of peace with them, and it shall be an everlasting covenant with them; I will establish them and multiply them, and I will set My sanctuary in their midst forevermore. My tabernacle also shall be with them; indeed I will be their God, and they shall be My people. The nations also will know that I, the LORD, sanctify Israel, when My sanctuary is in their midst forevermore."

—Ezekiel 37:21–28

Jeremiah speaks

Behold, I will bring back the captivity of Jacob's tents, and have mercy on his dwelling places; the city shall be built upon its own mound, and the palace shall remain according to its own plan.

—Jeremiah 30:18

Hear the word of the LORD, O nations…He who scattered Israel will gather him…for the LORD has redeemed Jacob, and ransomed him from the hand of one stronger than he. Therefore they shall come and sing in the height of Zion.

—Jeremiah 31:10–12

"I will bring my people Israel and Judah back from captivity and restore them to the land I gave their forefathers to possess.... Do not be dismayed, O Israel," declares the LORD. "I will surely save you out of a distant place, your descendants from the land of their exile.... 'O LORD, save your people, the remnant of Israel.' See, I bring them from the land of the north and gather them from the ends of the earth."

—Jeremiah 30:3, 10; 31:7–8, NIV

Zechariah speaks

"I am exceedingly angry with the nations at ease; for I was a little angry, and they helped—but with evil intent." Therefore thus says the LORD: "I am returning to Jerusalem with mercy; My house shall be built in it," says the LORD of hosts, "and a surveyor's line shall be stretched out over Jerusalem."

Again proclaim, saying, "Thus says the LORD of hosts: 'My cities shall again spread out through prosperity; the LORD will again comfort Zion, and will again choose Jerusalem.'"

—Zechariah 1:15–17

Jesus Rebuts Replacement Theology

Jesus was the greatest teacher of the ages. He gave us three sermons (Matthew 24, Mark 13, and Luke 21) that are prophetic in nature. These passages present the events of the future in chronological order from the time he delivered them until his Second Coming. In Matthew 24, the disciples ask Jesus three questions:

1. "When shall these things be?" This question referred to the destruction of the temple that he and the disciples had just left. Jesus answered in Luke 21:20, "But when you see Jerusalem surrounded by armies, then know that its desolation is near." This was accomplished in A.D. 70 when the Roman general Titus destroyed Jerusalem.

2. "What will be the sign of your coming?"

3. "And of the end of the age?" This world as we know it is coming to an end in spite of the faulty theology that says the church is going to become so victorious we will usher in the Millennial Age. Paul says in Galatians 1:4, "...that He [Jesus Christ] might *deliver us* from this present evil age, according to the will of our God and Father" (emphasis added).

Let's move to Matthew 24:15, where Jesus is describing the Great Tribulation that will come upon the earth. This verse assumes that Israel is "home" and in control of the holy places. "Therefore," Jesus told them, "when you [the Jews] see the 'abomination of desolation,' spoken of by Daniel the prophet, standing in the holy place..."

The "holy place" is the temple in Jerusalem, and according to this verse, the Jews are in control of the temple. How could they control the temple without being in control of Jerusalem? How could they be in control of Jerusalem if they were replaced?

Jesus continues by saying, "Then let those who are in Judea flee to the mountains" (Matthew 24:16).

Judea is part of what is now called the West Bank. Jesus's statement assumes that in the last days the Jews would be living on the West Bank. Jesus is describing in verses 16–20 a general evacuation of the population in and around Jerusalem from a military attack.

Jesus is saying, "When this military attack happens, don't go to Jerusalem, which is five minutes away, for safety. You have less than five minutes to save your life. Flee to the mountains as a matter of civil defense."

Then he tells them:

> Let him who is *on the housetop* not come down to take anything out of his house. And let him who is *in the field* not go back to get his clothes.
>
> —Matthew 24:17–18, emphasis added

The roofs in Israel then and now are flat. People store things on the roof and sometimes sleep there. There is an outside stairway to the ground. Jesus is saying, "When this military attack happens, don't carry anything down from the roof. Just run for safety!"

The fields in Israel were within eyesight of the house. Jesus said, "When this happens, don't even go to the house to get your clothes." Why? There won't be time.

Think of the situation in Israel today. There is not much time for the people to flee from incoming Katyusha rockets launched by Hezbollah or other terrorist groups in Lebanon or Syria. The rockets take less than five minutes to reach Jerusalem.

Jesus continues with this:

> But woe to those who are pregnant and to those who are nursing babies in those days! And pray that your flight may not be in winter or on the Sabbath.
>
> —Matthew 24:19–20

Why mention the grief or sorrow of those who are pregnant or with nursing babies? Because their escape would be much more difficult. Why pray that your escape does not take place in winter? For the same reason; it would be far more difficult.

Why pray that your flight not be on the Sabbath? This verse again assumes that religious Jews are in control of the government in Israel and the laws of the Sabbath are being strictly enforced. On the Sabbath in Israel, everything shuts down! There is no transportation. Even the elevators in the hotels and high-rise apartments shut down unless run by electronic control.

A Hamas or Hezbollah rocket attack upon Jerusalem at a time when there is no transportation and when even the elevators are shut down would lead to a disaster.

Jesus confirms that these terrible days of tribulation will occur when the Jews are back in Israel:

> And unless those days were shortened, no flesh would be saved; but *for the elect's sake* those days will be shortened.
>
> —Matthew 24:22, emphasis added

The elect in this verse are the Jewish people.

If the prophets and Jesus were certain that Israel would return to the land, if they were certain that Israel had not been cast aside and replaced in the economy of God, how is it that America's replacement theologians can't see it? Perhaps it is the blindness of narcissistic arrogance.

The Old Covenant Is Not Dead

Replacement theology advances the concept that the Old Covenant, or Old Testament, has been replaced by the New Testament. In many churches, the Old Testament is presented in a manner that suggests it is an inferior approach to God. It is offered as a record of harsh, legalistic justice without mercy that fosters fear without compassion. The intimation is that it should be disregarded by New Testament Christians who have superior light and love.

Need we be reminded that the loving theology of the New Testament, as translated by the Roman church fathers, is what sponsored the Crusades, the Inquisition, and ultimately produced the Holocaust?

Replacement theologians tell us, "The Old Covenant must likewise be put to death. God cannot, will not, has never before and never will be in covenant with more than one people."[8]

Is that what the Bible teaches? Certainly not. This is a misstatement used to promote anti-Semitic lies in the church. To respond to others who present this erroneous statement to you, it is important to begin with an explanation of biblical covenants.

What Is a Covenant?

In the Bible, the meaning of *covenant* is wrapped up in the Hebrew word *berith*. It means a contract, a will, a testament, or a bond. A covenant in Scripture cannot be revoked, altered, annulled, or replaced by a new covenant. A new covenant can enhance, extend, or complement the former covenant, but it never replaces the former covenant.

The Old Testament is God's will concealed; the New Testament is God's will revealed. The Word of God begins at Genesis 1:1, not Matthew chapter 1.

A covenant is not to be confused with a vow. A vow can be broken by certain conditions of revocation. A covenant, once spoken into existence, is everlasting.

Three kinds of covenant are recorded in the Scripture:

1. Shoe covenant (Ruth 4:7)
2. Salt covenant (Leviticus 2:13; Numbers 18:19)
3. Blood covenant (Genesis 15:7–18; Matthew 26:28)

The shoe covenant

The most common type of covenant was the shoe covenant. Whenever someone in Israel wanted to enter into a contract to perform a specific task, he would give his shoe or sandal to the person entering into the covenant with him.

If you have been to Israel, you know that it's impossible to go very far without your shoes. The terrain is covered with sharp, jagged rocks and blazing hot sand. The first time I was in Israel,

I knew immediately why stoning was the method of capital punishment. Rocks are everywhere! All you have to do is look down, and you will find plenty of rocks.

When you gave your shoe to someone on this rocky terrain in an act of covenant, you were saying, "I won't be far from this spot when you come looking for me."

When Boaz came before the elders to redeem Ruth from her close relative, he took off his sandal and gave it to the relative and expressed his desire to marry Ruth. This was the shoe covenant in Israel.

The salt covenant

The salt covenant was a covenant of loyalty. Salt was carried by everyone in Israel in a small pouch tied to the belt. When the sun's heat caused a loss of body salt through perspiration, the individual would take a pinch of salt to prevent muscle cramps.

The salt covenant was made by the contracting parties as they reached into their respective pouches to get a pinch of salt to exchange with the person entering into the covenant. As they exchanged salt by placing it in the other person's pouch, they would recite the contents of the covenant they were making. It was unthinkable in Bible times for those who entered the salt covenant to be disloyal to each other even if they had been bitter enemies. Their covenant of loyalty was expressed by saying, "There is salt between us!"

After exchanging salt, they would shake their individual pouches to thoroughly mix the grains of salt. The significance of this covenant was that as long as the grains of salt were mixed, the contract was in effect. Technically, the only way the contract could be terminated was for each of the contracting parties to retrieve their exact grains of salt from the other person involved. Of course, this was impossible once the salt pouches were ceremoniously shaken.

Historically, Jewish people have preserved their friendships with each other by invoking a covenant of shared salt. When sitting at a meal together, a dish of sea salt was passed around, with each person at the table taking a pinch of salt in the palm of their hand and eating the salt at the same time. Some still practice this tradition today as a symbol of friendship, and it means that everyone who is participating is right with each other and with God.

When a Jewish person needs to resolve a dispute with a family member or friend, he invites the person into his home to share a dish of salt. Each person licks his finger and dips it in the salt, or puts a pinch of salt in the palm of his hand, and then both people eat the salt in their hand at the same time. This symbolizes that the salt has healed the wound in their relationship, just as salt heals the wounds of the body.

The blood covenant

The third kind of covenant in Scripture was the blood covenant. It was used only for the most urgent contracts. It consisted of dividing the carcass of an animal or animals in half and placing the halves on the right hand and left hand, making an aisle between them. The persons entering into this most serious covenant walked back and forth between the pieces of the sacrifice and recited the contents of the covenant. The symbolism, as expressed by the animal whose blood had been spilled and whose body had been split in half, was that if either party broke the covenant, their blood should be spilled and their body split in half.

There are two significant blood covenants recorded in the Bible. The first was between God and Abraham, giving Abraham and his descendants the land of Israel forever. The second was the shed blood of the Lamb of God at Calvary, removing the curse of sin from all humanity.

God's Blood Covenant With Abraham for the Royal Land Grant of Israel

When God passed the title deed of Israel to the descendants of Abraham, Isaac, and Jacob forever, he did so with the most spectacular blood covenant recorded in the Old Testament.

> Then He [God] said to him [Abraham], "I am the LORD, who brought you out of Ur of the Chaldeans, to give you this land to inherit it."
>
> And he said, "Lord GOD, how shall I know that I will inherit it?"
>
> So He said to him, "Bring Me a three-year-old heifer, a three-year-old female goat, a three-year-old ram, a turtle dove, and a young pigeon." Then he brought all these to Him and cut them in two, down the middle, and placed each piece opposite the other; but he did not cut the birds in two. And when the vultures came down on the carcasses, [Abraham] drove them away.

> Now when the sun was going down, a deep sleep fell
> upon [Abraham]; and behold, horror and great darkness
> fell upon him.
>
> —Genesis 15:7–12

The contracting parties in this blood covenant were Jehovah God and Abraham. Abraham slew the heifer, the goat, the ram, and the birds and laid their carcasses out on the ground, preparing to enter into the blood covenant concerning the land of Israel. God instructed Abraham to slaughter and divide many animals because this was to be the most important real estate covenant in the history of mankind. It would be a covenant that nations would contest and theologians would condemn.

At sundown, God caused Abraham to fall into a "deep sleep." It was probably the same divine anesthesia he used on Adam when he removed a rib to form Eve in the first-recorded organ transplant (Genesis 2:21). It was necessary for God to put Abraham in a "deep sleep," for no man can look upon God and live.

> And it came to pass, when the sun went down and it was
> dark, that behold, there appeared a smoking oven and a
> burning torch that passed between those pieces. On the
> same day the LORD made a covenant with [Abraham],
> saying: "To your descendants I have given this land, from
> the river of Egypt [Red Sea] to the great river, the River
> Euphrates..."
>
> —Genesis 15:17–18

In his sleep, Abraham saw "a smoking oven and a burning torch" that passed between those pieces. In the Old Testament, the burning torch signified the presence of the Shekinah glory of God. God himself, apart from Abraham's participation or promise, was binding himself in a blood covenant to fulfill that which he had promised to Abraham. The dimensions of the land are clearly stated as being from the Nile River to the Euphrates River and from the Persian peninsula to Asia Minor.

If God has broken his blood covenant with Abraham, as replacement theologians are teaching, what confidence can we have that he will keep the blood covenant of the cross? Both covenants were made by the same God. If God is a covenant breaker, he lied to Abraham and to David. If God is a covenant breaker and has cast aside the Old Covenant for the New Covenant, how can we be sure he won't cast aside the New Covenant? If God is a covenant breaker, every Bible believer on Planet Earth can go to bed tonight not knowing that our sins are forgiven, not knowing the blood sacrifice of the Lamb of God at Calvary was valid, and believing the biblical text is utter rubbish composed by a God who cannot keep His word. That is the message of replacement theology. I reject that message!

God's Covenant With Abraham
Creating the Nation of Israel

The Abrahamic covenant was restricted to the seed of Abraham through Isaac and Jacob. This covenant established Israel as a nation and is *everlasting and unconditional. Unconditional* means this covenant is contingent upon God's faithfulness to Israel, not Israel's faithfulness to God. God says five times in this covenant, "I will, I will, I will." He never says to Abraham, "You must...you must!" The covenant reads:

> Now the LORD had said to [Abraham]: "Get out of your country, from your family and from your father's house, to a land that *I will* show you. *I will* make you a great nation; *I will* bless you and make your name great; and you shall be a blessing. *I will* bless those who bless you, and *I will* curse him who curses you; and in you all the families of the earth shall be blessed.
>
> —Genesis 12:1–3, emphasis added

The seven specific sections of this covenant are:

1. A land that I will show you
2. I will make you a great nation
3. I will bless you
4. I will make your name great
5. You shall be a blessing
6. I will bless those who bless you and curse him who curses you
7. In you all the families of the earth shall be blessed.

An Unconditional Covenant

The Christians who now say that God broke his covenant with Israel are ignoring the scripture written by King David. He says the covenant was unconditional.

> If his sons [the Jews] forsake My law, and do not walk in My judgments, if they break My statutes, and do not keep My commandments, then will I punish their transgression with the rod, and their iniquity with stripes. Nevertheless My lovingkindness will I not utterly take from him, nor allow My faithfulness to fail. My covenant will I not break, nor alter the word that has gone out of My lips. Once I have sworn by My holiness; I will not lie to David. His seed shall endure forever, and his throne as the sun before Me; it shall be established forever like the moon, even like the faithful witness in the sky. Selah.
>
> —Psalm 89:30–37

Jehovah God promised Israel that if they broke his statutes, his commandments, and his law, he would punish them with a rod and stripes. The pages of history are laden with the anguish of the Jews. They have passed under the rod of God's judgment, but his unconditional covenant holds.

God uses the sun and the moon as witnesses that the covenant with the Jewish people stands. The witness of the sun and moon is a twenty-four-hour reminder for anyone, anywhere on Planet Earth, who can look up and see the blinding light of the sun or the reflected light of the moon. As long as man can see either of these, Israel has a covenant with God.

Moses confirms that God keeps covenant forever:

> Therefore know that the LORD your God, He is God, the faithful God who keeps covenant and mercy for a thousand generations with those who love Him and keep His commandments.
>
> —Deuteronomy 7:9

God keeps covenant for a thousand generations! Technically speaking, a thousand generations is forty thousand years, but the reference is simply an expression of speech that emphasizes the meaning *forever*. God is a God of everlasting covenant. The God of Abraham, Isaac, and Jacob does not break covenant—*ever*!

The Old Testament Replaced?

Let me repeat that when something is replaced in the plan of God, it is plucked up by the roots, cast over the wall, burned, and buried, never to be heard of again. If the Old Testament is replaced by the New Testament, why do the Ten Commandments appear in the New Testament? By an honest investigation of Scripture, anyone can determine that nine of the Ten Commandments reappear in the New Testament. The fourth commandment, which refers to the Sabbath, is not found because the New Covenant permits any day to be observed as a day of rest and worship (Romans 14:5–6; Galatians 4:9–10; Colossians 2:14–17).

The following chart displays the New Testament scriptures

that incorporate the Ten Commandments of God as given through Moses and recorded in the twentieth chapter of Exodus.

The Ten Commandments in Both Old and New Testaments		
Commandment	**Old Testament**	**New Testament**
1. No other gods	Exodus 20:3	Matthew 4:10; 22:37–40; Luke 4:8
2. No carved images (idols)	Exodus 20:4–6	Romans 2:22 1 Corinthians 5:10; 6:9–11
3. Don't take the name of the Lord in vain	Exodus 20:7	Acts 26:11 Romans 2:24 Colossians 3:8
4. Remember the Sabbath	Exodus 20:8–11	(Law of the Sabbath not commanded in the New Covenant)
5. Honor your father and mother	Exodus 20:12	Ephesians 6:1–3 Colossians 3:20 2 Timothy 3:2
6. Don't murder	Exodus 20:13	Romans 13:9 1 Peter 4:15 1 John 3:15
7. Don't commit adultery	Exodus 20:14	Romans 2:22; 13:9 1 Corinthians 6:9–11
8. Don't steal	Exodus 20:15	Romans 2:21; 13:9 Ephesians 4:28 1 Corinthians 6:9–11 1 Peter 4:15

The Ten Commandments in Both Old and New Testaments		
9. Don't lie about your neighbor	Exodus 20:16	Romans 13:9 1 Peter 4:15
10. Don't covet what other people have	Exodus 20:17	Romans 13:9 1 Corinthians 5:10; 6:9–11

Again, if the Old Testament is dead, why are the commandments reconfirmed in the New Testament? If the Old Testament is dead, why did Jesus use it as a foundation for his teaching in his earthly ministry? Jesus said, "You shall love your neighbor as yourself" (Matthew 19:19). Where did he get that doctrine? It's a verbatim quote from Moses: "You shall love your neighbor as yourself" (Leviticus 19:18).

The apostle Paul continues to teach the law of love in Romans 13:9 with "You shall love your neighbor as yourself."

James echoes the theme by saying, "If you really fulfill the royal law according to the Scripture, 'You shall love your neighbor as yourself,' you do well" (James 2:8).

What is the source of these New Testament teachings? They come from Moses and the Old Covenant, which, according to replacement theology, is supposed to be dead, useless, and replaced.

Jesus Christ personally validated the divine authority of the Old Covenant by saying, "Do not think that I came to destroy the Law or the Prophets: *I did not come to destroy* but to fulfill" (Matthew 5:17, emphasis added). He continues in the next verse to declare that the Old Covenant would be valid "till heaven and earth pass away." Heaven and earth have not passed away; neither has the Old Covenant!

169

CHAPTER 11

ANSWERING SECULAR CRITICS

I N THIS CHAPTER I WANT TO ADDRESS THOSE READERS WHO are not Christians. As you know by now, I have very firm beliefs about the roles that Israel, the Jewish people, and the Middle East will play according to the prophecies foretold in the Bible. I have expressed these beliefs in my book *Jerusalem Countdown*. You may or may not agree with my religious beliefs, but we are free, as Americans, to have differing religious and political beliefs and to still live peacefully with each other, as a nation, and celebrate our differences. It is perfectly acceptable to agree to disagree.

That is the course that Aryeh Scheinberg and I have taken for more than twenty-five years now. The rabbi and I have become extremely close friends over the years, and I thoroughly enjoy those rare occasions when we have time to sit and talk about the Torah and world affairs. We agree on many, many things, but when it comes to the nature and identity of the Messiah, of course, we simply agree to disagree—with the understanding that when we stand in the streets of Jerusalem and see Messiah walking toward us, one of us will have a major theological adjustment to make!

Even if you do not agree with my religious beliefs, I hope you can agree that thousands of years of persecution and hatred of the Jewish people are absolutely wrong. Whether that hatred is being directed at Jews by the Christian church, Adolf Hitler, Osama bin Laden, Mahmoud Ahmadinejad, Hamas and Hezbollah, the Ku Klux Klan, or ordinary Americans in the privacy of their own homes and businesses, it is evil. It is anti-Semitism, and it is a sin that damns the soul. Call it what you will, it must be stopped at every turn. We absolutely cannot continue to ignore it.

Questions will surely arise, especially in the media, about my intentions for writing this book and for standing so strongly with Israel. I make no apologies for my staunch belief that Israel has every right to defend herself, including preemptive strikes against known terrorists and supporters of terrorism who have vowed to wipe Israel off the face of the earth. Let me emphasize that my efforts are not intended to create a conflict, but to deal with one that already exists—and to put it in the context of anti-Semitism and hatred, regardless of its source.

Whether that hatred and oppression emanate from the Christian church as it did for so many centuries; from radical Islamic fundamentalists, as it clearly does today; or from apathetic, politically correct, and disbelieving citizens of our own nation, who would rather look the other way when hatred is being justified for any reason, it is unacceptable. It is a moral imperative that everyone who believes we should treat others the way we wish to be treated, with basic civil and human rights, to take seriously the very real threat to Israel and the Jewish people that exists in the world today.

A number of critics have claimed that because I teach biblical prophecy, including a worldwide conflagration that will lead up to the final battle of Armageddon, that my intent is to ignite World War III and kick-start the Apocalypse. It's absolutely untrue. I hate war. I deplore the loss of life and the devastation caused by wars. When I speak about a coming conflict or worldwide war, it is something that has been predicted by the prophets of Israel for thousands of years. Now these ancient prophecies are becoming reality. My explaining prophecy in terms the average person can understand will not make any event come true. These prophecies are going to happen exactly as described in Scripture because their source is God Almighty. These prophetic events will happen at a time of God's choosing, not man's.

I would love for this book to open the eyes of every world citizen who will approach this subject with an open mind. Whether we are talking about the Middle East or our own neighborhoods, we cannot turn a blind eye to the history that is reality as it relates to Israel and the Jewish people. It is about helping people to see that anti-Semitism, and all other forms of religious hatred, make it impossible to agree to disagree peacefully.

In Defense of Israel is my call to action to support a people who have faced persecution at every turn and have been battling terrorism every day since May 15, 1948. It is my call for fifty million evangelicals to join forces with the five million Jews in America to stand up and speak up for Israel—that is a match made in heaven. We are spiritual brothers, and our future together should be one of compassion and cooperation until Messiah comes and the enemies of Israel are defeated and we enter the golden age of peace.

From the simple standpoint of our national interest in the world, Israel is a key component of the Middle East and should be supported regardless of differing religious viewpoints.

Israel Is a Vibrant Democracy

Israel is the only true democracy in the Middle East. It is an island in a sea of radical Muslims screaming for the death of every *infidel* (non-Muslim). Hamas has recently conquered the Abbas government and now represents a terrorist state a mere one thousand yards from the walls of Jerusalem. Hezbollah, the radical "party of God," occupies Lebanon, on Israel's northern border. Both Hamas and Hezbollah are funded, trained, and equipped by Iran and Syria. As I write this in June 2007, it is only a matter of time before a major war engulfs the Middle East and impacts the entire world.

In spite of the stress created by constant terrorism, Israel is a pluralistic democracy, with respect for human rights, and accords unprecedented rights to its Arab population. In fact, Arabs living in Israel have more freedom than they would have living in any other country in the Middle East. They have the freedom to become Israeli citizens with full voting rights. They have their own political parties and can elect members to the Knesset. Arab-language newspapers and Arab-owned businesses are thriving inside Israel.

Israel is also the nation in the Middle East where women have the most freedom. Author Tashbih Sayyed observed Muslim women "going to schools, colleges and universities without any restriction or inhibition....Such an open society is definitely a threat to the traditional Arab society in which women cannot be allowed any kind of freedom, as free and independent women in a traditional Muslim culture is a sign of diminishing male authority and respect."[1]

Sayyed further observed that "Arabs living under Muslim Arab authorities want to be treated in Israeli hospitals, when suffering from life-threatening illnesses." In spite of the ongoing conflict between the Palestinians and Israelis, no Israeli hospital "has ever refused treatment to any Muslim Arab, even in cases when the person who came for treatment was suspected of being a potential terrorist. The world knows that some of the Arabs who received treatments in Israeli medical facilities did in fact come back as homicide bombers, causing death and destruction to the innocent citizens of Israel."[2]

Is the converse true? Do Israelis living in other Middle East countries have similar rights and freedoms? Do they enjoy the same standard of living? Absolutely not. They are in grave peril living in Arab countries. Why can people not see the disparity and the hypocrisy?

Israel Is Not the Cause of the Middle East Conflict

It is propaganda that asserts that Israel has robbed anyone else of their land or that they are somehow the cause of the Middle East conflict. Opposition to Israel by the neighboring Muslim nations stems from their religious belief that Jews are infidels. Muslim children in elementary schools are taught that Jews come from monkeys and pigs. Dressed in military paraphernalia, these children learn to shout, "Death to the Jews!" and "Death to America!"

in unison. Teachers applaud these young children, who are taught from an early age to love death, hate Jews, and long for the glory of being a martyr.

One of the poison streams that sweep young Palestinians into such fanatical hatred is the claim that the Jews have taken their land from them. Not so!

The fact of history is that Israel lived as a sovereign nation in the land until the Roman army, led by Hadrian in A.D. 130, attacked Jerusalem. The emperor Hadrian hated the Jews for their monotheistic theology and their refusal to bow to Rome. Hadrian retaliated against the Jews by removing the name Judea from the maps of the world and renaming the area Syria Palaestina, after the ancient enemies of Israel, the Philistines. His attempt to rename Jerusalem as Aelia Capitolina failed miserably, but his efforts to steal the Jewish claim to the land of Israel were successful.[3] In spite of Hadrian's use of the term Palaestina, the Palestinians have *never* existed as an autonomous society, and the land of Israel *never* belonged to them. Media reports in America referring to Israel as an "occupier" have no basis in fact. It is nothing more than anti-Semitic propaganda.

In order to respond to distortions of truth about the true cause of the Middle East conflict, some basic facts of Israel's history must be understood, beginning at the end of World War I with the breakup of the Ottoman Empire, which had ruled the region for many centuries.

The Balfour Declaration and the British Mandate

The Balfour Declaration of 1917 was a letter written by British Foreign Secretary Arthur James Balfour to Lord Rothschild. It was a statement of policy that defined how the British government would divide the recently conquered Ottoman Empire. It also included language that formed the basis of the British position in support of a Jewish state in the area known as Palestine.

By 1922 significant conflict between Jews and Arabs in Palestine had caused Britain to rethink its policy on the region. The Churchill White Paper alludes to this changed mind-set. Then, in June of 1922, the League of Nations approved the *British Mandate* (the Palestine Mandate of the League of Nations), which specifically outlined Britain's responsibilities in Palestine, including the establishment of a Jewish national home. The document incorporated language from the Balfour Declaration in support of Jewish immigration and political status. However, it also stated that Britain could withhold the large territory east of the Jordan River, called *Transjordan* at the time, from Jewish settlement.

On September 11, 1922, the division of the land east and west of the Jordan River became official. The League of Nations approved a memorandum from the British government stating that Transjordan would be excluded from Jewish settlement. With that memo, British leaders initiated Israel's first "land for peace" offering, taking away 77 percent of the region originally mandated for the future Jewish state.

On May 15, 1923, Britain officially recognized Transjordan (now known as Jordan) as a state. That same year, Britain also transferred part of the Golan Heights to Syria, drawing protest from U.S. president Woodrow Wilson:

> The Zionist cause depends on rational northern and eastern boundaries for a self-maintaining, economic development of the country. This means, on the north, Palestine must include the Litani River and the watersheds of the Hermon, and on the east it must include the plains of the Jaulon and the Hauran. Narrower than this is a mutilation....I need not remind you that neither in this country nor in Paris has there been any opposition to the Zionist program, and to its realization the boundaries I have named are indispensable.[4]

Throughout the 1930s, the British drew back further and further from the pro-Zionist commitment of the Balfour Declaration, and in 1939 another British White Paper was issued. The White Paper of 1939 limited Jewish immigration into Palestine to a total of seventy-five thousand Jews over a period of five years. As a result of this limitation, scores of desperate Jews trying to escape Hitler's Holocaust in Europe were turned away. Many were even rounded up by the British as "illegal immigrants" and sent back by ship to Hitler and the death camps.[5]

Many Jews began to equate the cruelty of Hitler's regime with that of the British government's refusal to grant sanctuary to their countrymen. Rabbi Joseph Teluskhin, in his book *Jewish Literacy*, summarizes the perspective of the Jewish people regarding the White Paper of 1939 with these words:

> For Jews, the White Paper [of 1939] represents two things: the betrayal by England of its commitment to Zionism, and a clear message to Hitler that Britain really did not care what he did to the Jews.[6]

It was at this time that Menachem Begin walked onto the stage of Israel's history.

Menachem Begin and the King David Hotel

Recently released from years of incarceration in a Soviet prison, Menachem Begin went immediately to Palestine. Outraged by the British immigration policies in Palestine, Begin helped organize the *Irgun*, an underground military force whose purpose was to prevent the British from sending Jews without papers back to Hitler's Holocaust in Europe.

The daring exploits of the Irgun are well documented in Begin's book *The Revolt*. He became such a severe thorn in the side of the British that Great Britain placed a price on his head of $100,000 dead or alive.[7]

Menachem Begin is often labeled by the liberal media as a terrorist, but nothing could be further from the truth. Menachem Begin was a freedom fighter whose targets always consisted of British military personnel or those who were armed combatants against the Jewish people.

The truth about Menachem Begin and the bombing of the King David Hotel needs to be told. In July 1946, the King David Hotel was being used by the British army as a command post. British troops invaded the Jewish Agency in June 1946 and confiscated large quantities of documents. Information about Jewish Agency operations, including intelligence activities in Arab countries, was taken to the King David Hotel.

After news of a massacre of forty Jews in Poland reached him, Begin and the Irgun placed explosives from the basement through the top floors of the King David Hotel. Desiring to avoid civilian casualties, Begin placed three telephone calls—one to the hotel, another to the French Consulate, and a third to the *Palestine Post*—warning that explosives in the King David Hotel would soon be detonated.

The call to the hotel was apparently received and ignored. The commanding officer did not believe that the Irgun could have possibly placed explosives in the hotel under the noses of the British high command. The commanding officer made it very plain to Begin he had no intention of leaving the hotel, saying, "We don't take orders from the Jews." The King David Hotel exploded, leaving ninety-one people dead and forty-five injured. Among the casualties were fifteen Jews.[8]

The bombing of the King David Hotel was not an act of terrorism—it was an act of combat between warring forces. Shortly thereafter, England decided to leave Palestine, and the Jewish state was born. Mr. Begin and the Irgun laid down their arms along with the *Haganah* (a Jewish paramilitary group formed during the era of the British Mandate) upon the rebirth of the Jewish state on May 14, 1948.

Aware that seven Arab states under the leadership of former Nazi and British officers were about to attack them, the Jews of Palestine declared the establishment of the State of Israel on May 14, 1948, at

4:32 p.m. in a moving ceremony at the Tel Aviv Museum. The first Israeli prime minister, David Ben-Gurion, the George Washington of Israel, declared, "We hereby proclaim the establishment of the Jewish State in Palestine, to be called Israel."[9]

After reading the declaration of Israel's independence, Ben-Gurion announced the first decree of the new Jewish state: the White Paper of 1939, hated by the Jews for its curb on Jewish immigration and land sales, was made null and void.

The Six-Day War of 1967

When the Jews of Jerusalem were forced to surrender in the early phases of the 1948 Israeli War of Independence, they relinquished perhaps their greatest treasure—the sacred wall that encircled the Temple Mount, site of the two ancient, destroyed Jewish temples. The capture of the Western Wall by Israeli soldiers almost twenty-three years later during the June 1967 Six-Day War represents one of the most significant moments in Jewish history.

Six days hardly seems long enough to fight and win a war against five Arab nations, but the dramatic victory by the State of Israel between June 5 and June 10 is nothing short of miraculous. When the dust cleared on June 11, Israel found herself four times larger and in possession of some of Judaism's holiest sites. A mere two weeks earlier, the world had predicted the possible annihilation of Israel in the face of the combined armies of Egypt, Syria, and Jordan; now the Jewish state was regarded as the greatest military power in the Middle East.

Yes, Israel initiated the first strike in this war on June 5, but it was self-defense. Egypt's president Nasser had been announcing his plan to rid the world of the "Zionist entity" throughout the month of May. Then Nasser closed the Strait of Tiran to all Israeli ships, an act that constituted legal grounds to go to war, according to international law. Israel did nothing to retaliate, feeding Nasser's belief that they were weaker than the Arabs. By May 27, the rhetoric of the Arabs was eerily similar to that which we hear today:

> Our basic objective will be the destruction of Israel.[10]
> —Gamal Abdel Nasser, President of Egypt

> Our goal is clear—to wipe Israel off the map.[11]
> —Abdel Rahman Aref, President of Iraq

Knowing that these threats were real, we can easily see that Israel was acting in self-defense when she launched the preemptive air strike that took out the entire Egyptian air force (and most of Syria's) in one day.

At this point, it is important to note that the lands gained by Israel in the Six-Day War—the disputed territories of what is called the West Bank—were never part of a sovereign Palestinian nation. Jordan and Egypt had maintained possession of the area since 1948, when the British pulled out. Before that, the area was considered to be a part of the Ottoman Empire.

These lands were gained by Israel in 1967 in a defensive war. It is misleading to refer to these disputed areas as "occupied Palestinian territories," which implies that the area belongs to Palestinian Arabs and is being held captive by Israelis. Biblical arguments aside, it is still wrong to forget the three-thousand-year-old Jewish ties to the West Bank and Gaza that predate any other people group. It is wrong to deny that they were forced out of their land by invaders and have consistently maintained a desire to return to this homeland throughout history. They are entitled to possession of the land—not a renouncement of their claim to the land—in a final peace agreement.

The Yom Kippur War of 1973

In 1973, during the feast of Yom Kippur, Egypt and Syria joined forces in a surprise attack on the territories Israel had conquered six years earlier. Because they initiated the invasion on the Jewish holiday, the attacking armies were able to make significant advances at first. However, within a week, Israel was able to drive them back and regain all of the territory they had occupied before the war. This convinced Egyptian president Anwar Sadat that the Arabs could never defeat Israel in a war—no doubt a contributing factor in his willingness to sign the peace treaty with Israel at Camp David four years later.

Unlike the war of 1967, this time Israel's leaders feared international opposition and chose not to take preemptive measures when war seemed imminent. As a result, twenty-seven hundred Israeli soldiers lost their lives, many of them overwhelmed in the initial attack. Golda Meir resigned her position as Israel's prime minister a short time after the war, and in her autobiography, *My Life*, she confessed that she would regret this decision until the day she died.[12]

The Lebanese War

In the early 1980s Israel's war against the PLO forces along Lebanon's southern border was welcomed by then Israeli defense minister Ariel Sharon, who hoped to force a peace treaty between the two countries and put an end to the relentless shelling of Israeli settlements in northern Israel.

At first, most Israelis identified with the goals of the war, but similar to current changing of the tide of opinion in America right now regarding the war in Iraq, once Israel discovered that getting into Lebanon was easier than getting out, support for Israel's longest war waned. PLO fighters disbursed themselves among civilians, meaning that any attempt by Israeli forces to bomb the PLO inevitably meant killing innocent civilians as well. From around the world, Israel faced condemnation for attempts to bomb PLO strongholds, despite the attempts to keep civilian casualties at a minimum.

As soon as the Israelis were able to occupy Beirut, the PLO agreed to evacuate Lebanon, a significant, although short-lived, Israeli victory. The next event in the war—the election of Bashir Gemayel as Lebanon's new president—would prove to be the cause of its lasting controversy for Israel. Scholar and rabbi Joseph Telushkin, sums it up this way:

> Gemayel promised that he would sign a peace treaty between Israel and Lebanon when he took office. Days before his inauguration, however, he was assassinated by pro-Syrian terrorists. The Phalangist forces that Gemayel headed were outraged by the loss of their leader. The

following day, Israeli troops in West Beirut allowed Phalangist soldiers into the Palestinian refugee camps of Sabra and Shatilla, ostensibly to disarm the PLO terrorists remaining in the camps. Instead, the Phalangist soldiers carried out a massacre, killing about a thousand people, very few of whom were PLO fighters. Around the world, Israel was held responsible for the massacres: To this day, most Arabs believe that it was not the Phalangists who carried out the massacres, but the Israeli Army. An exasperated Prime Minister Begin said, 'Non-Jews killed non-Jews and the Jews are blamed.[13]

Operation Opera: the bombing of Baghdad's nuclear reactor

Earlier I described how Israel made a preemptive strike against Osirak, a nuclear reactor constructed by the Iraqi government eleven miles southeast of Baghdad in 1977. Fearing the reactor would be used to produce nuclear weapons, and with evidence that France was ready to ship fuel rods to activate the reactor, Israelis felt the nuclear facility was a direct threat and must be destroyed.

When diplomatic negotiations failed, Israel turned to military action to remove the threat and authorized an air strike called Operation Opera on June 7, 1981. The site was quickly knocked out of commission, significantly setting back Iraq's nuclear development program.

Israel suffered political fallout, with many governments, including the United States, criticizing the operation. Israel insisted that its actions were justified as self-defense. Menachem Begin explained that as long as the reactor remained in operation, he saw the people of Israel facing a peril similar to that posed by Adolf

Hitler. Although the United Nations condemned Israel's actions, most Jews understood why the reactor had to be destroyed: "Never again" could they allow enemies who had announced their intention to kill them gain access to weapons of mass death. Israel is to be congratulated for taking nuclear weapons out of the hands of Saddam Hussein.

It was as a result of this intense media attack on Israel that I decided to hold the first Night to Honor Israel in September 1981 to express our appreciation to the local Jewish community and to the nation of Israel. For twenty-five years we have conducted these nonconversionary celebrations to express support of Israel and the Jewish people. With the rapid growth of Christians United for Israel, these Night to Honor Israel events are now being conducted from coast to coast.

The Oslo Accords

The Declaration of Principles on Interim Self-Government Arrangements is often called the Oslo Accords because the document was finalized in Oslo, Norway, in 1993. The declaration was signed in Washington DC on September 13, 1993, by Yasser Arafat, representing the Palestinian Liberation Organization (PLO), and Shimon Peres, representing the State of Israel, in the presence of then U.S. president Bill Clinton and Israeli prime minister Yitzhak Rabin.

Since that accord, the various factions of the newly constituted Palestinian Authority have routinely committed violence against Israel. It is difficult to know, especially in light of current events, whether anyone in the PA has actually ever been willing or completely able to control these attacks. They are acts of terrorism, plain and simple. Israel has rightfully had to take steps to defend its citizens, just as we in the United States would do if attacked in a similar manner, in response to the terrorist acts. In every instance the intent of the Israeli government has been to comply with the Oslo Accords in ways that were deemed acceptable at the time of the agreement.

As I finish writing this book, civil war has broken out among the Palestinians living in Gaza, with the Hamas and Fatah parties locked in a violent battle for control of the government. Hamas, which is sworn to the destruction of Israel as a matter of policy, prevailed in Gaza, causing the surviving leaders of Fatah to flee; the West Bank remains under the control of Fatah.

It is clear that war is coming to Israel and the Middle East, but I am convinced of one thing: the nation of Israel will survive. This time the evangelical Christians of America will be standing side by side with the State of Israel and the Jewish people. When the last shot is fired in the Middle East, the flag of Israel will be flying over the ancient walls of Jerusalem.

For this reason I can confidently say, as I do in the next chapter, "Israel lives!"

CHAPTER 12

"ISRAEL LIVES!"

DURING THIRTY-PLUS YEARS OF MINISTRY I HAVE delivered quite a few sermons on the life of Joseph. One of the most popular was an eight-part series I preached called "Joseph's Journey: From the Pit to the Palace."

While we were laying the groundwork for Christians United for Israel, the story of Joseph kept coming to my mind. I've always taught that Joseph's life is a foreshadowing of the life of Christ. It's a rich analogy with far too many correlations to be coincidence. Their names even come from the same Hebrew root word, *Yeshua*, which can be translated into English as Joshua, Joseph, or Jesus.

Sitting in my office late one afternoon, after the phones had died down and the daily stream of appointments had been concluded, I picked up a pen and began to give expression to the thoughts that had been forming in my subconscious.

As I wrote, I sensed the Spirit of God expanding my understanding of the biblical story of old. It was more than a foreshadowing of the life of Christ. Rather, the lives of Jesus and Joseph present a prophetic overlay that describes the future relationship of Christians and Jews. Both lives are exact in their meaning in their own generation. In studying prophecy—or history, for that matter—you learn that it's possible to tell the future by knowing the past. By examining the life of Joseph and comparing it to the life of Jesus, you will have an exact compass for the future.

Take time to read through the following chart carefully. I put the material in this format because I want you to see these striking Bible parallels written side by side.

Joseph	Jesus
Beloved son: Joseph was the favorite son of his father.	*Beloved son:* Jesus was the only begotten son of God the Father.
Royal garments: Joseph was given a coat of many colors, a sign of royalty.	*Royal garments:* Jesus wore a seamless garment, a valuable piece of clothing, which the Roman soldiers gambled for at his crucifixion. He was hung as the "king of the Jews," and he is called in Scripture the "prince of peace."
Sent with food: Joseph was sent by his father to his brothers with food.	*Sent as food:* Jesus was sent from God the Father to the earth as the living water and the bread of life.
Rejected by his family: When Joseph arrived, he was rejected by his brothers.	*Rejected by his family:* When Jesus left the splendor of heaven and came to Earth as a man, he "came unto his own, and his own received him not" (John 1:11, KJV).

Joseph	Jesus
Sold as a slave: Joseph's brothers cast him into a pit and sold him into slavery.	*Sold as a slave:* Jesus Christ was betrayed by Judas for thirty pieces of silver, the price of a slave.
Falsely accused: When Joseph arrived in Egypt, he was falsely accused of rape by Potiphar's wife.	*Falsely accused:* When Jesus preached in Jerusalem, he was falsely accused by the Pharisees of being a drunkard, a heretic, and a demonized madman. Rome considered him an insurrectionist too dangerous to live.
Sent to prison: Joseph was sent to prison for several years but was divinely released after interpreting Pharaoh's dream. He was released from prison to stand at the right hand of Pharaoh, the most powerful man on the earth.	*Sent to prison:* Jesus was sent to the prison of death, from which he divinely arose on the third day to stand at the right hand of almighty God, the most powerful being in the universe.
Raised to power: Joseph was sent from prison because of his gifts of divine revelation. He was immediately brought into the palace as the prime minister, the right-hand assistant to Pharaoh, the most powerful man on the earth at that time.	*Raised to power:* When Jesus was crucified, he went into the prison of death, came out miraculously on the third day, and ascended to the throne at the right hand of God the Father, the most powerful person in the universe eternally.

Joseph	Jesus
Gentile heirs: Joseph was given a Gentile bride, who produced two heirs, Manasseh and Ephraim.	*Gentile heirs:* Jesus was given a Gentile bride at the cross. Like Manasseh and Ephraim, Gentile converts have been grafted into the original olive tree, whose roots are Abraham, Isaac, and Jacob (Romans 11:17).
Equal share: According to the Torah, Manasseh and Ephraim were given equal shares of land as an inheritance with the sons of Jacob.	*Equal share:* At the cross, Gentiles were given an equal share with the Jewish people. We are joint-heirs with Christ (Romans 8:17).
Three visits to the land: Driven by hunger, Joseph's brothers came into the land of Egypt three times to seek food.	*Three visits to the land:* Three times the Jewish people have come into the promised land of Israel: the first was the Exodus, under the leadership of Moses and then Joshua; the second was the end of the Babylonian exile, under the leadership of Nehemiah; and the third was on May 15, 1948, at the rebirth of the national homeland.
Blinded to true identity: Joseph's brothers came face to face with him but did not recognize him. They were blinded to his identity because he lived as an Egyptian and spoke to them through an Egyptian interpreter.	*Blinded to true identity:* Jesus Christ is the flesh-and-blood brother of the Jewish people (Matthew 25:40), but at this time they are blinded to his true identity (Romans 11:7, 10, 25, 32).

Joseph	Jesus
True identity revealed: On the third entrance into the land of Egypt, Joseph revealed himself to his brothers. First he ordered all of the Gentiles to leave the palace. Jewish historians say that Joseph proved his identity to his brothers by showing them his circumcision, which was not an Egyptian practice.	*True identity revealed:* Before Jesus Christ reveals himself to the Jewish people, the church will leave the earth in an event known as the Rapture. Jesus will prove his identity in the same way Joseph did: by showing signs in his flesh—not just the scars in his hands and feet, but also the one in his side, where a Roman soldier pierced his chest to make sure he was truly dead.
Weeping as a family: When Joseph's brothers recognized him for who he was, they fell on his neck and wept for joy.	*Weeping as a family:* When the Jewish people recognize Jesus for who he is—when they actually see him—"they will mourn as one mourns for his only son" (Zechariah 12:10).
Endowment of land: After he was reunited with his brothers, Joseph sent for his father and all the Jewish people who had survived the famine. He gave them the rich and fertile land of Goshen in Egypt.	*Endowment of land:* When Jesus returns to Earth as Messiah, the Jewish people will be given all of the historic land, and the Jewish people will be center stage in the eternal kingdom that is to come during the millennial reign. They are not now, nor have they ever been, replaced; they remain the apple of God's eye.

The biblical story of Joseph is not just a foreshadowing of Christ but of all that is going to happen at the end of time as we know it. Putting those two stories together is connecting the dots of the past with the world of tomorrow.

I began this book by mentioning the honor of being invited to address the 2007 Policy Conference of AIPAC, the American Israel Public Affairs Committee. That night some in the audience were stunned when I apologized for the many atrocities that had been committed against Jews throughout history in the name of Christianity. I spoke of the Crusades, the Spanish Inquisition, and, of course, the Holocaust.

"Where are the nations that have persecuted the Jewish people?" I asked the audience. "Where is Pharaoh and his army? Where are the Babylonians? Where are the Greeks, the Romans?

"Where is the Ottoman Empire? Where are that goose-stepping lunatic, Adolf Hitler, and his Nazi hordes? All are historic footnotes.

"But where are the Jewish people? They're alive and well; they're thriving; they're prospering; they're growing—"

The crowd began to stand to their feet and applaud.

"Even in the day of adversity," I continued, "they're still going forward.

"Where is Israel? Where are those who were scattered throughout the Diaspora? The mighty right hand of God has gathered them from the nations of the world, and Israel was miraculously born

May 15, 1948. Israel lives! Shout it from the housetop—Israel lives! Let every Islamic terrorist group hear it—"

People began to say it with me—"Israel lives!"

"Let every tin horn dictator in the Middle East hear it—Israel lives!

"Let it be heard in the halls of the UN—"

Their voices grew louder as they shouted with me—"Israel lives!"

"Let it echo down the marble halls of the presidential palace in Iran—Israel lives!

"Let it ring in the terrorist camps of Osama bin Laden—Israel lives! Israel lives! Israel lives!"

The room was electrified as we pronounced the verdict of the one who promised never to slumber or sleep as he watches over Israel: the chosen people of God are alive and well.

I've given similar speeches all over the country at our Night to Honor Israel events. I'm accustomed to an enthusiastic response, and our congregation at Cornerstone Church is even more vocal when they lift their voices in praise to God on a Sunday morning. But my heart was deeply stirred that night by the powerful current that rippled through the convention center.

Part of my emotion was the thrill of a scrawny eight-year-old boy from Channelview, Texas, who had watched his father weep at the rebirth of the nation of Israel—and who had grown up to proclaim God's love for the Jewish people in the corridors of influence. But mostly it was the bedrock knowledge that the message I had delivered was truth.

The Jewish people have suffered pogroms and persecution; they have outlasted Pharaoh's slavery and Hitler's Final Solution. And I have no doubt that long after Hamas and Hezbollah have been buried in the boneyard of human history, long after the crisis with Iran has been resolved, the flag of Israel will still be flying over the ancient walls of the sacred City of David, and Jerusalem will be the praise of all the earth.

NOTES

Chapter 1—It's 1938 . . . Again

1. *Reader's Digest,* December 1954, as quoted on Enotes.com, Famous Quotes: History, http://history.enotes.com/famous-quotes/an-appeaser-is-one-who-feeds -a-crocodile-hoping-it (accessed June 29, 2007).

2. Dwight D. Eisenhower, "I Shall Go to Korea" (speech, October 25, 1952, quoting Senator Arthur H. Vandenberg), http://www.time.com/time/printout/0,8816,8065 04,00.html (accessed July 2, 2007).

3. Elesha Coffman, "Final Solution, Part II," *Christian History Newsletter,* January 25, 2005, viewed at http://www.christianitytoday.com/history/newsletter/2002/ jan25.html (accessed June 29, 2007).

Chapter 2—My Lifelong Love for Israel

1. Truman Museum and Presidential Library, "Recognition of Israel Documents," http://www.trumanlibrary.org/whistlestop/study_collections/israel/large/ documents/index.php?pagenumber=3&documentid=49&documentdate=1948-05 -14&collectionid=ROI&groupid= (accessed May 30, 2007).

2. In United Nations parlance, Zionism is synonymous with racism. I use the term here in its original sense: a person who believes that Israel has a right to exist, that Jews have a right to return to Israel, and that Israel has the right to defend itself from behind definable borders.

3. TheKotel.org, "Facts and Figures: The Western Wall Tunnels," http://english .thekotel.org/content.asp?id=28, and "How the Temple Walls Were Built," http:// english.thekotel.org/content.asp?id=29 (accessed June 29, 2007).

Chapter 3—Sins of the Fathers

1. Gil Kaplan, *Israel's History of Persecution* (N.p.: n.d.), 23.

2. Edward H. Flannery, *The Anguish of the Jews* (Mahwah, NJ: Paulist Press, 1985), 51.

3. Ibid., 93.

4. Elinor Slater and Robert Slater, *Great Moments in Jewish History* (New York: Jonathan David Publishers, 1998), 162.

5. Eternal Word Television Network, "Canon 68: Jews Appearing in Public," Fourth Lateran Council, 1215, translation taken from Decrees of the Ecumenical Councils, Norman P. Tanner, ed., http://www.ewtn.com/library/COUNCILS/ LATERAN4.HTM (accessed July 2, 2007).

6. Ibid.

7. TheHistoryPlace.com, "Hitler Named Chancellor," *The Rise of Adolf Hitler,* http://www.historyplace.com/worldwar2/riseofhitler/named.htm (viewed July 1, 2007); TheHistoryPlace.com, "Nazis Boycott Jewish Shops," *The Triumph of Hitler,* http://www.historyplace.com/worldwar2/triumph/tr-boycott.htm (accessed July 1, 2007).

8. Guido Kisch, *The Jews in Medieval Germany* (Chicago: University of Chicago Press, 1949), 203.
9. Rabbi Joseph Telushkin, *Jewish Literacy* (New York: William Morrow and Company, Inc., 1991), 191.
10. Cecil Roth, *The Spanish Inquisition* (New York: W. W. Norton & Company, 1996); also BibleTopics.com, "The Spanish Inquisition," http://www.bibletopics .com/biblestudy/64.htm (accessed August 19, 2005).
11 Malcom Hay, *The Roots of Christian Anti-Semitism* (New York: Freedom Library Press, 1981), 166.
12. *Encyclopedia Judaica,* vol. 3 (Jerusalem: Keter Publishing House, 1978), 103.
13. Malcolm Hay, *The Roots of Christian Anti-Semitism* (New York: Freedom Liberty Press), 169.
14. Dagobert D. Runes, *The War Against the Jew* (New York: Philosophical Library, 1968), 114.
15. Information in this chart is taken in part from J. E. Scherer, *Die Rechtsverhaltnisse der Juden in der deutsch-osterreichischen Landern* (Leipzig, 1901), pages 39–49.
16. Hay, *The Roots of Christian Anti-Semitism*, 3.
17. John Toland, *Adolf Hitler*, vol. 1 (Garden City, New York: Doubleday & Company, Inc., 1978), 326.
18. Ibid., vol. 2, 803.
19. *Trial of the Major War Criminals before the International Military Tribunal*, vol. 1, (Nuremberg, Germany: International Military Tribunal, 1947), 50.
20. Ibid., 251.
21. Ibid., vol. 3, 439.
22. Ibid., vol. 8, 318–319.
23. Toland, *Adolf Hitler*, vol. 1, 233.
24. Sam Ser, "What Will Follow 'the Best Pope the Jews Ever Had'?" *Jerusalem Post,* April 3, 2005, http://www.jpost.com/servlet/Satellite?pagename=JPost/JPArticle/ ShowFull&cid=1112494793946 (accessed August 19, 2005).

Chapter 5—The Peoples of the Middle East

1. I have addressed the subject of divine election in full in my book *Jerusalem Countdown* (Lake Mary, FL: FrontLine, 2006, 2007).
2. SimpletoRemember.com, "World Jewish Population," http://www.simpleto remember.com/vitals/world-jewish-population.htm (accessed on March 17, 2007).
3. Ibid.
4. Central Intelligence Agency, *The World Factbook*, https://www.cia.gov/library/ publications/the-world-factbook/.
5. Ibid.
6. Palestinian Central Bureau of Statistics, *Statistical Abstract of Palestine No. 5*, http://www.pcbs.gov.ps/Portals/_pcbs/PressRelease/abstract_e.pdf (accessed July 5, 2007).

7. Central Intelligence Agency, *The World Factbook*, https://www.cia.gov/library/publications/the-world-factbook/.

8. Wikipedia.org, s.v. "Taliban," http://en.wikipedia.org/wiki/Taliban (accessed July 5, 2007).

9. Central Intelligence Agency, *The World Factbook*, https://www.cia.gov/library/publications/the-world-factbook/.

10. Ibid.

Chapter 6—The Religions of the Middle East

1. George W. Braswell Jr., *Islam: Its Prophet, Peoples, Politics and Power* (Nashville, TN: Broadman & Holman Publishers, 1996), 44.

2. Mark Gabriel, *Jesus and Muhammad* (Lake Mary, FL: Charisma House, 2004), 147.

3. Information taken from Braswell, *Islam: Its Prophet, Peoples, Politics and Power*, 44–48; Daymond R. Duck, *The Book of Revelation* (Nashville, TN: Thomas Nelson Publishers, 2006), 152–153.

4. Quoted on authority of Ibn 'Abbas in Sahih of al-Bukhari; attested by numerous Islamic scholars. See, for example, http://www.bibletopics.com/BIBLESTUDY/96a.htm and http://www.giveshare.org/islam/index.html.

Chapter 7—Revolution and Radical Islam

1. Anti-Defamation League, Major Terrorist Attacks in Israel, http://www.adl.org/israel/israel_attacks.asp (accessed June 25, 2007).

2. *Journal of Turkish Weekly*, "Iran: UN Ignores Israeli Threats to Tehran," June 19, 2007, http://www.turkishweekly.net/news.php?id=46190 (accessed June 25, 2007).

3. Associated Press, "Egypt Urges World to End Palestinians' Isolation," *International Herald Tribune*, March 17, 2007, http://www.iht.com/articles/ap/2007/03/17/africa/ME-GEN-Egypt-Palestinian.php (accessed July 5, 2007).

4. Associated Press, "Hamas-Fatah Gov't Seeks End to Boycott," USA Today.com, March 17, 2007, http://www.usatoday.com/news/world/2007-03-17-palestinians_N.htm?csp=34 (accessed July 1, 2007).

5. Reuters.com, "Thousands March to Protest Iraq War," March 17, 2007, http://www.reuters.com/article/newsOne/idUSN1726712200703178pageNumber=2 (accessed July 1, 2007).

6. *The 9/11 Commission Report: Final Report of the National Commission on Terrorist Attacks Upon the United States* (Washington: Government Printing Office), available at http://origin.www.gpoaccess.gov/911/.

7. Boaz Ganor, "The Islamic Jihad: The Imperative of Holy War," February 15, 1993, Jerusalem Center of Public Affairs, http://www.jcpa.org/jl/saa31.htm (accessed July 5, 2007).

8. MideastWeb.org, "The Covenant of the Islamic Resistance Movement (Hamas)," Article 13, http://www.mideastweb.org/hamas.htm (accessed July 1, 2007).

Chapter 8—Our Debt to the Jewish People

1. Adolf Hitler, *Mein Kampf,* Ralph Mannheim, ed. (New York: Mariner Books, 1999), 65.
2. Abraham Cohen, *Everyman's Talmud* (New York: Schocken Books, Inc., 1949), 73.
3. William J. Federer, *America's God and Country: Encyclopedia of Quotations* (Coppell, TX: FAME Publishing, 1994), 660.
4. Ibid., 388.
5. Ibid., 668–669.
6. Scholars usually point to Isaiah or Jeremiah (or both) as the compiler(s) of 1 and 2 Kings.
7. Mark Twain, "Concerning the Jews," *Harper's Magazine* (1899), as recorded in Mark Twain, *The Complete Essays of Mark Twain* (New York: Doubleday, 1963), 249.
8. Central Intelligence Agency, *The World Factbook,* https://www.cia.gov/library/publications/the-world-factbook/.
9. The National Archives Experience, "Declaration of Independence," http://www.archives.gov/national-archives-experience/charters/declaration_transcript.html (accessed July 2, 2007).
10. Joseph Telushkin, *Jewish Literacy* (New York: Harper Collins, 1991, 2001), 199.
11. National Park Service, "Hayme Salomon," The American Revolution: Lighting Freedom's Flame, http://www.nps.gov/revwar/about_the_revolution/haym_salomom.html (accessed July 2, 2007).
12. Emma Lazarus, "The New Colossus," *The Poems of Emma Lazarus* (1889), vol. 1.
13. Answers.com, "Albert Einstein," http://www.answers.com/topic/albert-einstein?cat=health (accessed July 2, 2007).
14. "Facts About Israel," as posted online by Israel21c, http://www.israel21c.org/bin/en.jsp?enPage=BlankPage&enDisplay=view&enDispWhat=Zone&enDispWho=DidYouKnow&enZone=Facts (accessed April 3, 2007).
15. Ibid.
16. Ibid.
17. Ibid.

Chapter 10—Answering Christian Critics

1. Hay, *The Roots of Christian Anti-Semitism,* 24.
2. Ibid., 26.
3. Runes, *The War Against the Jews,* 42.
4. Hay, *The Roots of Christian Anti-Semitism,* 9.
5. Ibid.
6. Earl Paulk, *To Whom Is God Betrothed?* (Atlanta: K. Dimension Publishers, 1985), 40.
7. Ibid., 47.
8. Ibid., 3.

Chapter 11—Answering Secular Critics

1. Tashbih Sayyed, "Israel's Arab Citizens and the Jewish State," *Islam Watch* Web site, http://www.islam-watch.org/TashbihSayyed/Muslim-Citizens-Jewish-State .htm (accessed June 22, 2007).
2. Ibid.
3. BibArch.com, "Colonia Aelia Capitolina," http://www.bibarch.com/glossary/MI/ ColoniaAeliaCapitolina.htm (accessed July 3, 2007).
4. Meir Abelson, "Palestine: The Original Sin," *Nativ* 97, no. 2: (March 2004).
5. Menachem Begin, *The Revolt* (New York: Dell Publishing, 1951, 1978).
6. Telushkin, *Jewish Literacy*, 287.
7. Begin, *The Revolt*, 70.
8. Jewish Virtual Library, "The Bombing of the King David Hotel," http://www .jewishvirtuallibrary.org/jsource/History/King_David.html (accessed July 2, 2007).
9. The Avalon Project at Yale Law School, "Declaration of Israel's Independence, 1948," http://www.yale.edu/lawweb/avalon/mideast/israel.htm (accessed July 2, 2007).
10. Telushkin, *Jewish Literacy*, 309.
11. Ibid.
12. Ibid., 318.
13. Ibid., 332.

INDEX

Planet Earth is on the verge of a geopolitical tsunami.

Want to know more about what is happening in the Middle East today? If you liked **In Defense of Israel**, you will love **Jerusalem Countdown**.

978-1-59979-089-3 / $14.99

John Hagee is back with a revised and updated edition of his best-selling book that you can't afford to miss.

Visit your local bookstore.